MARSILIO CLASSI

LETTERS FROM A NEW WORLD

AMERIGO VESPUCCI'S DISCOVERY OF AMERICA

Edited and with an introduction by Luciano Formisano

Foreword by Garry Wills

Translated by David Jacobson

Marsilio

New York

Luigi Ballerini, SERIES EDITOR

Vespucci's LETTERS I, II, III, IV, and VI translated from *Lettere di Viaggio,* edited by Luciano Formisano, Milan: Mondadori Editore. Copyright © 1985 L. Formisano. LETTER V translated from *Raccolta di documenti e studi publicati dalla R. Commissione Colombiana pel Quarto Centenario dalla scoperta dell'America,* Rome, 1892–96.

FOREWORD copyright © 1992 Garry Wills.

INTRODUCTION translated from *Nuovo Mondo. Gli italiani,* edited by P. Collo and P.L. Crovetto, Turin. Copyright © 1991 Giulio Einaudi Editore, reprinted with the permission of the publisher.

LETTER OF COLUMBUS TO HIS SON, LETTER OF NATURALIZA-TION OF VESPUCCI, LETTER OF APPOINTMENT OF VESPUCCI AS "PILOT MAJOR," EXCERPTS FROM NAVARRETE'S *COLECCIÓN DE LOS VIAJES,* AND EXCERPTS FROM LAS CASAS'S *HISTORY OF THE INDIES,* are reprinted from *Letters of Amerigo Vespucci and Other Documents Illustrative of His Career,* edited and translated by Clements R. Markham, London: The Hakluyt Society, 1894

EXCERPTS FROM WALDSEEMÜLLER'S *COSMOGRAPHIAE INTRODUCTIO* are reprinted from *The Cosmographiae Introductio of Martin Waldsemüller,* by Joseph Fischer, S.J., and Franz Von Wieser, edited by Charles G. Herbermann, United States Catholic Historical Society, 1907.

All illustrations are reproduced with the kind permission of the New York Public Library.

Copyright © 1992 Marsilio Publishers, Corp.
853 Broadway, Suite 1509
New York, New York 10003

HC ISBN 0-941419-62-2
PB ISBN 0-941419-63-0

TABLE OF CONTENTS

FOREWORD
by Garry Wills

Why is it not called the continent of South Columbia, of North Columbia? Why not the United States of Columbia? It is true that Columbus never touched the soil of the future United States. But neither probably did Amerigo Vespucci, whose first name *was* applied to the whole new hemisphere Columbus had stumbled on.

At least Columbus *was* the first of his European contemporaries to make the crossing. And he commanded his own expeditions, sailing four times to the land he was exploring. Vespucci came shortly after, as pilot in squadrons commanded by others, and the number of his voyages is disputed. Early in the sixteenth century Bartolomé de Las Casas was complaining of the injustice that gave Columbus' prize to Amerigo.

But Columbus *had* named what he reached—the Indies. It was not a new name because he did not think he had found anything new. And his misnomer has stuck. We still speak of the West Indies, and call the indigenous people Indians. Admittedly, we have to distinguish *American* Indians from natives of India—once again, Amerigo intrudes himself.

Columbus broke into a place whose existence had been unsuspected in Europe. But it was so unsuspected that Columbus could not recognize the enormity of his own adventure. He sailed athwart a mystery, but he was entering this "new world" with a very *old* world map in his mind, and no encounters with the unexpected could jolt that map quite out of his head.

Columbus believed, partly on the basis of Biblical texts, that the globe was girdled by one large land mass, whose extremities—the Azores off Portugal and the islands off Japan—were separated by one comparatively small ocean.[1] Even when Columbus came to suspect—on his third journey—that he was moving in areas not reported on by travelers to the Orient, he felt this was a land south of the Asiatic land mass. This left undisturbed the general disposition of the globe's land (filling most of the surface) and water (one "ocean river" running around the land mass). The reports of Vespucci first led Europe to suspect the momentous truth—that there are two oceans, and what Columbus had hit was a separate continent isolated on either side by these oceans.

Columbus was the last of the great medieval explorers. Though he lived in the Renaissance, he participated in few of its intellectual interests. He worked for the most retrograde monarchs of his time, who were conducting the Spanish Inquisition and "cleansing" the Iberian peninsula of all Moors and Jews. Columbus hoped to use the gold of the Orient to fund a new Crusade for recapturing the tomb of Christ in Jerusalem.

Columbus came from the Genovese working class and had a catch-as-one-can education, strong on practical skills, weak on Latin and literature. Vespucci came from the Florentine professional class, like his contemporary, Machiavelli. The Vespucci family had strong ties of service to the ruling Medici family. Amerigo grew up in the circle of artists like Vasari and Botticelli, of poets like Ariosto and Poliziano, of thinkers like Marsilio

[1] The debate Columbus had with Spanish officials was over the *size* of the globe. No one, contrary to a myth enshrined by Washington Irving, believed in a flat earth. Columbus drastically underestimated the size of the globe, in defiance of the best scientific opinion of his time.

Ficino and Machiavelli. Amerigo's uncle was a famous monk, the scholar Giorgio Antonio Vespucci, Botticelli's patron. Amerigo remembers being tutored by Fra Giorgio Antonio, along with Piero Soderini, who became the principal ruler in the Florentine Republic after the death of Lorenzo de' Medici (the Magnificient). Machiavelli was Soderini's protégé (enemies called him Soderini's puppet). One of Vespucci's two famous public letters was addressed to Soderini, and it recalls their school days together under Fra Giorgio Antonio.[2]

Vespucci entered public life as a secretary on a diplomatic mission to France, serving the Medici government—the same role Machiavelli would play under the Republic. But in 1492 Lorenzo the Magnificient died. That was the *annus mirabilis* in which Columbus reached his West Indies, a Spaniard (Alessandro Borgia) was elected Pope, the Moors were defeated at Granada—and Amerigo went to Spain. He was there to serve the Medici banking interests, and he soon became involved in the financing of Columbus' second expedition. He had a scholarly as well as a commercial interest in the exploration—as an astronomer, he was intrigued by inventions that promised to make celestial navigation more scientific.

Columbus sailed "by the seat of his pants." He was a master dead-reckoner (one who estimates position by combining direction and estimated surface speed). This made Columbus a kind of patron saint to amateur yachtsmen like Samuel Eliot Morison. Vespucci, working with instruments still hardly up to the task, was interested in finding out what he had encountered and where it was—he did not take as many things for granted as Columbus did.

Vespucci's second certain trip across the Atlantic (called his

---

[2]See page 58 below.

third in the public letters) overlapped with Columbus' fourth voyage. Both men were seeking the same thing—the gold of the Indies, lying behind the frustrating outer "islands" so far encountered. Columbus thought he could sail through the "outworks" he had been dealing with. Vespucci planned to sail south and get around the obstacle (whatever it was). As he went farther and farther south, down the long coast of what is now Brazil, he became convinced this was a "new world," heavily populated, off all maps as they had been conceived to that point.

But this "new world" was not enough to change the basic logic of the earlier maps. Columbus, too, had thought he found something new to the south of "Asia." This would add an extension *below* the known land mass. It would not, of itself, shake the centrality of that single mass.

The language of Vespucci's first public letter is compatible with the idea of a "new world" under and subordinate to the known configuration of lands. But in his second published letter, Vespucci treats the southern and northern parts of the area he and Columbus explored as a single continent *that is not Asia*. This was a stunning breakthrough in the state of knowledge, one Columbus never achieved. What separated this continent from Asia? Vespucci gives no definite answer, but he was computing distances that approximated the real size of the globe, and a natural supposition—soon made specific on the Waldseemüller map of 1507—was that *another* mass of water separates the mysterious continent from Asia.

Waldseemüller himself credited Vespucci with the information that led to the first cartographic suggestion that the Pacific Ocean exists. He even put what purported to be a portrait of Vespucci above the new continent, to balance the figure of Ptolemy presiding over the "old world" of prior geography. And

Waldseemüller put a form of Vespucci's first name (Latinized into "America") on the land we know as Brazil. The name would later be extended to the whole "new" continent, despite some later misgivings on Waldseemüller's part.

Vespucci, like Columbus, is a man of mystery. Since he did not raise, outfit, and command his own expeditions, but "piggy-backed" on others, there is less record of his journeys than of Columbus'. His second known journey was undertaken with Portuguese, not Spanish, sponsorship. The two public letters known in his day spoke of four journeys, one before and one after the certifiable ones, matching the Columbian record. When the three unpublished letters were found in the eighteenth century, they were used to undermine the authenticity of the public ones.

Vespucci, a Florentine of that city's devious heyday, had many purposes. Unlike Columbus, he had patronage in a number of quarters, with the Medici as with the Spanish and Portuguese courts. Like Columbus, he had propaganda purposes in his published writings. Undoubtedly he also kept some information to himself for future use. But he was trusted by the Spanish monarchs, who made him their chief of navigation (piloto mayor), an important post ever since Portugal had set up its "command center" of nautical information. Vespucci was in charge, in effect, of "mission control" for space exploration when he died—unlike Columbus, who died in disgrace, fighting for his outdated visions and unreaped benefits. Each played an indispensable role in breaking out of the geographical confinement of the Western world: but when it comes to naming the new, one must know that it *is* new. Vespucci, however hazily, did.

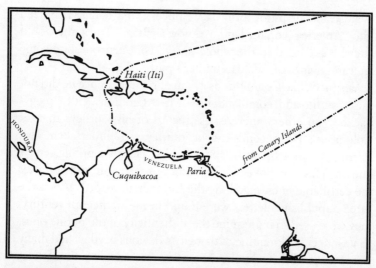

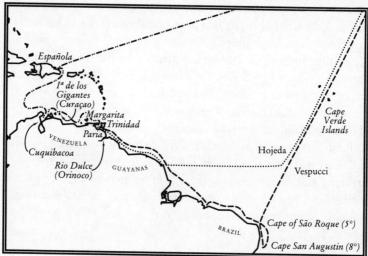

Top: *First voyage*
Bottom: *Second voyage*

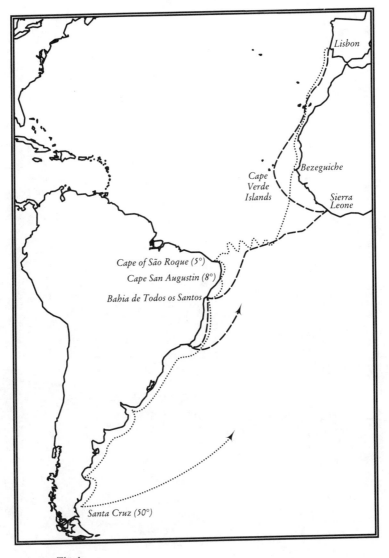

Lisbon

Bezeguiche

Cape
Verde
Islands

Sierra
Leone

Cape of São Roque (5°)
Cape San Augustin (8°)
Bahia de Todos os Santos

Santa Cruz (50°)

.... Third voyage
-------- Fourth voyage

INTRODUCTION
by Luciano Formisano

Apart from some documentary references, Amerigo Vespucci's "American" experience is summed up in the handful of letters attributed to him, of which there are two main groups: A) accounts printed during the navigator's lifetime; B) "familiar" letters which circulated only in manuscript form.

A) includes:

I. The *Mundus Novus*: A Latin translation of a lost Italian original, attributed to a "iocundus interpres" who has been identified, though not conclusively, as the Veronese humanist and architect fra' Giovanni del Giocondo.

The letter was sent from Lisbon to the patron of his Florentine years, Lorenzo di Pierfrancesco de' Medici (of the "Popolani" branch of the family). It refers to a voyage undertaken at the behest of King Manuel I of Portugal (1495-1521), along the coasts of South America to 50 degrees south, clearly with the objective of searching for the passage to the southwest toward the Moluccas opened up by the southern latitude Cabral had reached a year earlier. Weighing anchor from Lisbon on 14 May 1501, the fleet is said to have made a landing near Bezeguiche (Cape Verde), thereafter heading south-southwest; in particular, the landing on terra firma in a region that lay between Venezuela and Brazil is said to have taken place on 7 August, and the return to Lisbon on 22 July

1502.[1] On the whole the letter corresponds in substance to the second and third "familiar" letters (cf. below).

Although there are discrepancies in its account of coastal explorations, the letter is categorical in identifying the lands discovered as a "New World." The label is ambiguous, but the editor used it to mean precisely "unknown land," even if some other loaded meaning might be readily deduced from the degree determined for the remotest latitude, and from the effort to devise a "geometrical" representation of the new-found land. In particular, the parcelling out of geographical and ethnographical material into distinct sections and the recourse, through description of the southern sky, to a rudimentary iconographic apparatus, reflect the desire for scientific exposition that is already apparent in the writer's very choice of diction: a scholastic sort of Latin, quite slipshod and primitive, yet perfectly consistent with the antiquated Gothic character of the printing, and still adequate to assure this brief work an international circulation. In this sense the pamphlet fully belongs to the tradition inaugurated by *De insulis in mari Indico nuper inventis*, the Latin version of Columbus's letter announcing his discovery, completed on 29 April 1493. But one can also point out an intermediary link in the chain, *De insulis meridiani atque Indici maris nuper inventis*, an account by Guillermo Coma of Columbus's second voyage up to the return of Antonio de Torres, rendered into Latin by Niccolò Scillacio of Messina, a professor at Pavia, where the book was printed on 13 December 1494. In any case, the *Mundus Novus* enjoyed an immediate and lasting renown much on the order of Columbus's *De insulis*. It was published, without typographical notes, maybe in Florence, at the end of 1502 or the beginning of

1 Cf. Magnaghi 1924, I, p. 34.

1503 (the death of its addressee on 20 May of that year provides a terminus ante quem), and was then reprinted several times in the course of a few weeks, over an area spanning Venice, Paris, and Antwerp. It met with particular success in the German-speaking countries, where there was no lack of commercial enterprises directly interested in the recent discoveries. The Augsburg edition of 1504, the first to bear a date, was followed by those of Cologne, Nuremberg, Strasbourg, Rostock, and translations into German (Nuremberg, 1505) and Flemish (Antwerp, 1506-1508?). In Italy the celebrated letter will come into prominence again with the *Paesi novamente retrovati et Novo Mondo da Alberico Vesputio Florentino intitulato* [Countries Recently Discovered And Called by A.V. the New World]: the second among the Italian travel anthologies concerning America and Portugal edited by Fracanzio da Montalboddo, a professor of rhetoric at Vicenza, where it was printed on 3 November 1507. Fracanzio's compilation, reprinted no less than seven times throughout the sixteenth century, was then retranslated into Latin by the monk Arcangelo Madrignano (*Itinerarium Portugallensium*, Milan, 1508), thus providing the basis for a translation back into vernacular by Mathurin Redouer de Sendacour, which was printed in Paris as early as 1515. Another Italian version, enriched by various learned details that cannot be traced to the Latin original, was finally prepared by Giovanni Battista Ramusio for the first volume of the *Navigationi et Viaggi* (Venice, 1550).

The declaration of a "New World" and the pseudoscientific apparatus were undoubtedly captivating. The success of the work could only have been enhanced by the novelty of the ethnographic material, identical in substance to that of the third familiar letter (see below), but duly peppered with observations, more crude than they were savory, about the promiscuity and the sexual extravagances of the natives.

2. The *Lettera di Amerigo Vespucci delle isole nuovamente trovate in quattro suoi viaggi* [Letter of A.V. Concerning the Isles Newly Discovered on His Four Voyages] (cited as *Lettera* [Letter]). Printed in Florence perhaps in 1505,[2] it is addressed to a "Magnificent Lord," whom Ramusio and two manuscripts identify as Piero di Tommaso Soderini, Gonfalonier of Justice, the head, that is, of the Florentine Republic up until 1512, the year in which he was dismissed from office: a thoroughly plausible recipient, both because of the place left empty by Vespucci's former patron (Lorenzo having died the year before), and because of the political and familial ties binding Soderini to the branch of the Popolani. Add to this the Gonfalonier's known curiosity about travel tales[3] and the detail which the text so conveniently emphasizes, that Soderini was a pupil of Amerigo's uncle.

In signing off in his letter to Lorenzo di Pierfrancesco, the author of the *Mundus Novus* had not forgotten to mention the two voyages he had undertaken on mandate of the King of Spain, alluding at the same time to his preparations for a fourth voyage (the second of those backed by Portugal). Thus the novelty of the *Lettera* was anticipated, it being in fact presented as an organic exposition of Vespucci's voyages between 1497 and 1504: four, like those of Columbus, but equally divided between Spain and Portugal.

---

2 If not 1504, given the type of Antonio Tubini and Andrea Ghirlandi (or as common opinion would have it: of Piero or Bernardo Pacini, the printer being Giovanni Stefano di Carlo of Pavia).

3 Attested to by Giovanni da Empoli's *Vita* for Girolamo da Empoli, his uncle: cf. M. Spallanzani, *Giovanni da Empoli, mercante navigatore fiorentino* [Giovanni da Empoli Merchant Seafarer of Florence], Florence, 1984, pp. 103-4.

In particular, the two Spanish voyages correspond on the whole to the account given in the first familiar letter (see below), though they are compressed into a rather dubious chronological and geographical order. This is evident above all in the account of the first voyage (10 May 1497-15 October 1498), where certain observations about Venezuela and the island of Haiti (*Iti* in the text) are related to an expedition supposedly made between 16 and 38 degrees north (between the coast of Honduras and Chesapeake Bay). There follows an altogether unlikely circumnavigation of the Yucatán, the Gulf of Mexico, and Florida, while the identifying of the mainland would have to have been set back to 1497, thus challenging Columbus's primacy.

Of the two Portuguese voyages, that of 1501-1502 corresponds to the expedition recounted in the *Mundus Novus* and in the second and third familiar letters (see below), but with the addition of certain definitely original details, such as the discovery and naming of the Cape Saint Augustine and of Bahia de Todos os Santos. Not so for the voyage of 1503-4, traditionally identified with the expedition of Gonçalo Coelho, which has no parallel in the corpus of the familiar letters, and above all is incompatible with the news of Amerigo's reentry into Spain from October 1502.[4] In addition, the voyage has evident points in common with the corresponding one by Columbus, which also culminated in a shipwreck; it also bears analogies with the voyage of 1492, for even the shipwreck of the *Santa María*, on 25 December of that year, followed upon the building of a fortress (that of Navidad) to defend the men left behind there.

A text as popular as it is erudite, the letter combines a first-

4 According to the testimony of Piero Rondinelli, in a letter of 3 October 1502, in *Raccolta*, III, II, p. 121.

person travel account with a scientific treatise, not without slipping into the fictional devices of an adventure yarn.[5] The double register is already apparent in the work's successful reception. On the one hand, it is a report in vernacular entrusted to a mediocre typographer, undoubtedly intended for the broad public with its love of travel tales and *mirabilia*, and who in fact quickly bought up the entire edition, at least to judge from the fact that five copies remain of it. On the other hand, it exists in Latin translation (*Quattuor Americi Vespuccij navigationes*) by the German Martin Waldseemüller (Hylacomilus), who included it as a work of geographical revision in a *Cosmographie Introductio*, that is, in a geography and cosmography manual, printed at Saint-Dié of Lorraine on 25 April 1507. This was largely the work of Waldseemüller himself, but also collaborated upon by the scholars belonging to the local "Gymnase Vosgien." The letter's intended recipient was identified as René, the second duke of Lorraine and of Bar, nominal King of Jerusalem, and protector of the Gymnase; although the reference to the dedicatee's study under Giorgio Antonio Vespucci was not removed from the text. In addition, the Latin version of the letter, translated into German as early as 1509, later resurfaced in the *Novus orbis regionum* of Simone Grineo (Basel, 1532) and the Florentine printing did not manage to suppress a separate manuscript tradition, represented today by three documents, one of which appears heavily corrupted and contains author's variants.[6] With these additions the number of manuscripts rises to five, if one considers the independence of

---

5 As the 16th-century writer Matteo Bandello shows, when he draws inspiration for novella XXXIV from Part I (cf. Formisano 1987, p. 228, note 67).

6 This is the so-called Amoretti copy, now in the Library of Congress, Washington, D.C.

both the Waldseemüller and the Italian version introduced by Ramusio in the first volume of his *Navigationi et Viaggi*, where the narration is limited to the third and fourth voyages, and combined with the Synopsis (*Sommario*) taken from the *Mundus Novus*.

There is an apparent difference, in both the fate of reception and physical appearance, in the three familiar letters addressed to Lorenzo di Pierfrancesco de' Medici, rediscovered and published only in the eighteenth century.[7]

B) includes:

1. The letter from Seville, written on 18 (or 28) July 1500, concerning the voyage made between 18 May 1499 and June 1500 by Alonso de Hojeda and Juan de la Cosa, on which Vespucci is said to have served as "pilot" (that is, as astronomer and cartographer): one of the numerous expeditions undertaken in the same years to the "land of Pearls," where Columbus had landed on 31 July 1498, on his third voyage. The account, of which six manuscripts survive, itself corresponds to the two Spanish voyages of the *Lettera*, particularly to the second voyage, with whose chronology and route it partially coincides.

2. The letter from Cape Verde, dated 4 June 1501: having come down to us in a single copy from the Riccardiano codex 1910, it refers to the first part of the Portuguese voyage detailed in the next letter, but also alludes to another missive, no longer extant, sent from Lisbon to the same person on 8 May 1501.

---

7 The first and third, presented respectively by A.M. Bandini *(Vita e Lettere di Amerigo Vespucci*, Florence, 1745) and F. Bartolozzi *(Ricerche istorico-critiche circa alle scoperte di Amerigo Vespucci*, Florence, 1789 [Historico-critical Research in the Discoveries of A.V.], and the second by Count G.B. Baldelli Boni *(Il Milione of Marco Polo*, Florence, 1827).

It tells of how the fleet, setting sail from Lisbon on 13 May 1501, sailed for Cape Verde, where it allegedly crossed with two ships that formerly belonged to the fleet of Pero Álvares Cabral, then returning from India. In this sense, the letter serves as an account of the voyage made by the discoverer of Brazil along the coasts of Africa and Asia, on the basis of the testimony, explicitly cited, of Gaspar da Gama (or da India), a converted Jew from Alexandria, Egypt, formerly in the company of Vasco da Gama. Important for a whole set of hitherto unknown facts (we find in it the first description of Malayan junks), the letter ends with the mention of the Florentine Gherardo [dal] Verde, the brother of Simone dal Verde, of whom we possess two letters relating to the second and third voyage of Columbus, and the probable bearer of the letter to Lisbon, if not also directly to Florence.

3. The letter from Lisbon, undated but definitely written after 22 July 1501, when Vespucci is said to have returned to Portugal. Preserved in two manuscript copies, the letter takes up the narrative of the second familiar letter by describing the Portuguese voyage from Cape Verde to the reentry into Lisbon.

The account presumably draws on the twenty-seven days spent among the Tupí-Guaraní tribe of Brazil, and is of considerable ethnographic interest. There is scant geographical information, on the other hand, which has to be indirectly deduced from cartographical tradition and from the few supplementary data contained in the *Lettera*. Here, of course, as in the *Mundus Novus* and in the *Lettera*, the most significant accomplishment is recorded: the latitude of 50 degrees south, which will again be reached (and surpassed) only with Magellan's expedition.

We are dealing, then, with three private letters, though they are so only through the fiction of an exclusive addressee; rather, they are "familiar" (though not "plain") letters, whose range of data, of economic as well as scientific import, is intended for a well defined circle of humanist merchants, both in Florence and in the "Florentine colonies" of Seville and Lisbon. This explains the characteristics of the writing, guided by a selective and paratactic memory that combines the old Florentine and mercantile tradition of the "book of memories" and the "commercial letter" with the genre of the pilot's logbook and the Baedeker-like records of Marco Polo, the Portuguese, and Columbus. This selectivity is obvious in the first familiar letter, whose literary craft is greater than the geographers are apt to admit, yet which in itself is meant to illustrate, by way of commentary, a map and a planisphere. This generic debt is evident in the letter from Cape Verde, the most reminiscent of Marco Polo's writing, and thus the least like Columbus's, in the entire corpus of letters. Finally, the physiognomy of the manuscript tradition can be accounted for: six codices of definitely mercantile origin, behind which one can glimpse the active presence of "our fellow Florentines" in Seville and Lisbon, readers who are not merely ideal, but also actual purveyors or forwarding agents to Florence. This is demonstrated especially by Riccardiano manuscript 1910, the famous collection of voyage accounts, most of them from a Portuguese context, compiled by the Pisan-Florentine Piero Vaglienti (1438-1514), a figure especially associated with the Sernigi and the Marchionni. Another example of these links: Giannotto Berardi, who first gave work to and eventually became an associate of Amerigo (and of Columbus) at Seville, began his activity as a merchant and slave trader while working as an agent for Bartolomeo Marchionni in that city.[8] In any case, we have here a "book" typically mercantile

---

8 But Vaglienti also had dealings with Guidantonio Vespucci and with the Appiani (the family of Semiramide, wife of Lorenzo di Pierfrancesco de' Medici): on this

down to its very appearance, where the dispatches, letters, and accounts of merchants and travelers, with their strongly idiomatic flavor, are arranged according to the chronological order in which they reached the compiler: and all of it introduced by an extract from Marco Polo, demonstrating the continuity of the medieval tradition and of the two registers, practical and fantastical, in this genre. But this basic premise remains valid also for Riccardiano codex 2112-bis: an anthology of voyage chronicles whose only extant pieces are the first familiar letter of Vespucci and the letter from Vasco da Gama's first voyage, which was formerly attributed to Amerigo, but should definitely be credited to Girolamo Sernigi (1453-1510), a Florentine merchant living in Lisbon, who later sailed on the Portuguese ships bound for Malacca. Finally, of the four other codices that have given us the first familiar letter, at least three come from Casa Strozzi, which is not surprising, since the Strozzi family's commercial dealings with the Iberian Peninsula are well known.

THE "VESPUCCI QUESTION"

The "public" character of the *Mundus Novus* and of the *Lettera* was enough to secure Amerigo's reputation. One contribution that was fundamental in this regard was the *Cosmographiae Introductio*, which, updating Ptolemy with Vespucci, twice proclaims the primacy of the Florentine in discovering a continent henceforth identified as the fourth part of the world: to be called, precisely, "Amerige[n], quasi Americi terra[m], sive America[m]." Concurrently, the name America (pronounced with

---

merchant-writer, cf. the introduction to P. Vaglienti, *Storia dei suoi tempi (1492-1514)*, edited by G. Berti, M. Luzzati, E. Tongiorgi, Pisa, 1982.

stress on the next to last syllable)[9] is printed on the planispherical map which in the appendix to the volume outlines the newly discovered lands. Here it refers exclusively to the part of the South American continent that corresponds to present-day Brazil and which a narrow strait separates from the region of Paria (Venezuela). The map thus helps to sanction an act of name-giving for which Amerigo does not seem to have been directly responsible, but which is based upon two texts attributed to him, where the ambiguous declaration, of a "New World" is clinched by the primacy of his landing on terra firma (in 1497). The same occurs with the titling of the *Paesi novamente retrovati et Novo Mondo da Alberico Vesputio Florentino intitulato*, a work that postdates the *Cosmographia* by some few months. The part of the book reserved for Vespucci gives new meaning to the extent of Columbus's discoveries on his first three voyages, which do in fact come earlier, according to the version supplied in the *Libretto di tutta la navigatione de' Re de Spagna et terreni novamente trovati* [Book of All Navigations of the Kings of Spain and the New-Found Lands] (Venice, 1504): unquestionably the first of the Italian travel anthologies to deal with "American-istic" matters.

Be that as it may, the Latin translation of the *Lettera*, irrevocably associated with the *Cosmographia*, was quite soon considered a direct attack on Columbus: an attack all the more treacherous for having been launched after the discoverer's death (20 May 1506), when his merits were already being questioned. This explains the violent reaction of Bartolomé de Las Casas, who viewed the *Lettera* (which he knew only in its Latin version) as a

9 Cf. G. Contini, "Vespucci e il nome dell'America," now in Idem, *Ultimi esercizi, ed elzeviri (1968-1987)*, Turin, 1988, pp. 221-25.

patent fake, a work of the same Vespucci who arrogated to himself "the discovery [. . .] of the continent, usurping the glory owed to the Admiral, its true artificer": for the new continent should have been called "not America," from Amerigo, but rather "Columba, from Colón or Colombo who discovered it, or the Holy Land or Land of Grace, the name he himself imposed upon it" (*Historia*, I, p. 374b). The so-called "Vespucci question" begins here: the question of which voyages the Florentine actually made, especially the first. This most polemical of questions was fed by nationalistic resentments and originated within the framework of the *Pleitos colombinos*, the lawsuit brought several times against Columbus's heirs by the Royal Treasury Office. And note too that calm, close examination was directly countered by the large or small lies, and the thousand evasions, of a text often unbearable in its magniloquent tone.

But a genuine "Vespucci question" arises only after the publication of the three familiar letters, with which the problem of the voyages made by the navigator takes on a textual, or rather, attributive meaning. It is a question for which there are therefore four distinct solutions: either all the letters are 1) authentic or 2) apocryphal; or the only authentic one is 3) the "public" series or 4) the familiar series. If the second hypothesis is no more tenable than the third, the first requires the acknowledgement of serious textual alterations not to be restricted to changes of dates and directions. Conversely, the fourth and final solution, first advanced by Alberto Magnaghi in 1924, and later defended with ingenious conviction and tenacity by Giuseppe Caraci and Marcondes de Souza,[10] has its merit in its elegance of argument and

10 Cf. G. Caraci, *Questioni e polemiche vespucciane*, Rome, 1955-6, 2 vols.

historiographic concreteness: what is fundamental is the celebratory character of the printed series, the only one in which Amerigo could directly rival Columbus in the number of voyages and in the primacy of his landing on mainland. Unless one is prepared to admit that the future "piloto mayor" of Spain, the official entrusted with examining and instructing Spanish pilots, composing and updating the "Padrón real" (the offical, secret map of the discovered lands), may be responsible for the incongruencies, the platitudes, the downright errors in geography that mar the *Mundus Novus* and above all the *Lettera*. Whence the idea of a double falsification: initiated with the presumed Latin version of a lost Vespucci text (a text that casts no doubt on the question of his priority, but in which the notion of four voyages appears for the first time), and complemented by the letter to Piero Soderini. Here the assemblage of already known materials, derived from the familiar letters and from the travel literature, and not only the American part, extends the scope of the similar procedure already presented in the *Mundus Novus*, which is itself used to advantage. And in fact it would be no accident if in the *Lettera*, where the anecdotal substance of the first "familiar" letter is divided between the first two Spanish voyages, the narrative increasingly picks up pace, ending in a shipwreck that recalls the one Columbus suffered on his fourth voyage, but also serves to mask the embarrassment of a counterfeiter running short of material. All is sealed by an excessively Iberianized diction, pointing up the scant likelihood of such supposed 'firsts' as the discovery of the continent in 1497, and the exploration of the central and North American coast up to the latitude of 38

_____

("Memorie Geografiche," Serie II, II-III), and Th. O. Marcondes de Souza, *Amerigo Vespucci e suas viagens,* São Paulo, 1954/2.

degrees north. Thus we can discern the general outline of a cultural and political operation, exquisitely Florentine in character, which glorifies Vespucci by indirectly attacking Columbus: this may suffice for an easily satisfied public, for whom the geographical discoveries are of interest primarily as a frame for marvelous facts, but not at Seville or Lisbon. From there, precisely, come the anti-Vespuccian attacks: idle and unjust, since the Florentine's merit remains that of having traversed, in only two voyages, the entire coast of southern America from the mouths of the Rio Magdalena (Colombia) at a latitude of fifty degrees south, anticipating Cabral in the discovery of Brazil (which he reached in 1499), and opening the route up to the subsequent expeditions which with Magellan would lead to the southwest passage.

The hypothesis is economical and elegant, even if it may also be tipped too heavily in regard to the facts—in favor, that is, of a nautical expertise amply documented by the appointment as "piloto mayor" and by the echoes of the Portuguese voyage in contemporary cartography. It is an expertise which in the first place one should keep from translating directly into skill as a sailor, much less a captain—something the Florentine apparently never was, earning the glory of having two continents named for him more by his rationalizing of data (let us say, of astronomic and cartographic knowledge), than by his nautical intuition. What must be avoided above all are certain captious arguments on the part of Magnaghi, pretending that once and for all they fill the gap between the order of the writing and that of the facts. Indeed, as far as the question of intertextual comparisons are concerned, not only are these not absent in the first familiar letter, but they fit perfectly within a literary genre founded by Columbus, with its remote antecedents in Marco Polo and his updated literary heirs, the Portuguese voyagers.[11] This is the only key to interpretation when it is put in the perspective of the narrative; only this can explain the sudden change of hand within the same body of "familiar" letters, when in the one from Cape Verde the unmentioned baxos of Guiana or Venezuela give way, in the knowing, Marco Poloesque style of a Lusitanianed Alexandrian Jew, to the ancient, fabulous bazaars of the Far East. Essentially, even if we admit that the letter to Soderini represents an extreme or borderline case, source criticism reveals a semiotic operation considerably more complex than that presupposed by a merely documentary perspective. The pathological repetitiveness of the two series of letters admits of a whole set of minimal "variants," gratuitous, often recontextualized, as would befit accounts that make no claim to exhaust once and for all an experience communicable only through fragments. In addition, the falsity of assemblage does not necessarily reflect on the sources; they are not in fact reducible to the three familiar letters, and thus do not exclude other Vespucci letters no longer extant. The congruence, or rather, the complementarity of the printed and the handwritten series would otherwise be incomprehensible, on the stylistic and the narrative as well as the linguistic level. Since, as it is unlikely that the Iberianizing diction of the Letter is entirely the product of an outright counterfeit especially if it is of Florentine origin (there are numerous terms that are rare or seen for the first time or appear side by side with few, but significant, Americanisms), the plain Tuscanizing of the second and third familiar letter is in fact contradicted by the letter of 1500, where the systematic purism of the Vaglienti codex finds a corrective in the exotic exuberance of Riccardiano 2112-bis. What remains elusive, then,

11 Cf. Formisano 1987 and 1991.

is basically the extent of the assemblage, but not, however, the presence of at least two hands, one of which definitely belongs to Vespucci. As is therefore demonstrated by the fragment discovered and published by Roberto Ridolfi,[12] the reply to a lost letter from Lorenzo di Pierfrancesco de' Medici, from which we can deduce the existence of a version similar but not identical to that of the third familiar letter. Now, the textual history of the fragment is not different from that of the private series: it has been transmitted thanks to a labor of copying; it lay hidden in a library until 1937. Furthermore, the text actually defines itself as a "familiar letter" and in the small copybook that contains it (which belonged to an old servant of the Casa Strozzi) it was transcribed from a copy of the letter of July 1500. There is a unique and instructive exception to this: the account of the Portuguese voyage goes back to the tradition of the four voyages, in particular to the form this tradition takes in the *Mundus Novus* (an allusion to the two Spanish voyages and an account of a Portuguese expedition), while the details unknown to the third familiar letter find a parallel (not without some contradictions) in the letter to Soderini. Magnaghi believes that this can be explained by a new textual adulteration subsequent to the Florentine printing,[13] whereas it might more simply be a case of a link in the chain leading from the

---

12 Cf. R. Ridolfi, "Una lettera inedita di Amerigo Vespucci sopra il suo terzo viaggio" [An Unpublished Letter of A.V. Concerning His Third Voyage], in *Archivio Storico Italiano,* XCV, 1937, vol. I, I, pp. 3-20. The codex is now at the Library of Congress in Washington, D.C.

13 Cf. A Magnaghi, "Una supposta lettera inedita di Amerigo Vespucci sopra il suo terzo viaggio" [An Alleged Unpublished Letter of A.V. Concerning His Third Voyage], in *Bollettino della R. Società Geografica Italiana,* Serie VII, vol. II, 1937, pp. 589-632.

Mundus Novus to the *Lettera*, which would draw upon at least one second account of Vespucci's Portuguese voyage.

In this precise sense, anyone who approaches the "question" without prejudices will find that the *Mundus Novus* and the *Lettera* should be regarded as texts that might best be labelled not pseudo- but rather para-Vespuccian.

VESPUCCI'S LIFE

Amerigo Vespucci was born in Florence on 9 March 1452 (or 1454), the third of five children of ser Nastagio di Amerigo Vespucci, notary of the Money-Changers' Guild, a resident of the District of Santa Lucia d'Ognissanti, and of Lisa di Giovanni Mini. From the Trecento on the Vespucci, who originally came from the surrounding countryside, owned houses in the Ognissanti quarter. The Ognissanti church, by the Hospital of San Giovanni di Dio (which was founded around 1380 by Simone di Piero Vespucci), contains the family chapel; however, the branch to which Nastagio belongs does not seem to have been especially well-to-do. In 1478-80 Amerigo is in France in the retinue of his distant relative Guidantonio Vespucci, Lorenzo de' Medici's ambassador to the Court of Louis XI. Returning to Florence, he enters the service of Lorenzo di Pierfrancesco de' Medici, the "Popolano" (cousin of the Magnifico), for whom he acts as an administrator both in the city and in the estates of Cafaggiolo and Trebbio del Mugello. By 10 March 1492 Vespucci has already traveled to Seville, assigned the task of overseeing the management of the bank of Lorenzo di Pierfrancesco de' Medici, newly headed by Giannotto Berardi. As a merchant and outfitter of the Atlantic fleets of the Crown, Berardi forms a partnership with Columbus, whose first expedition he finances. The company is gradually expanded to include Vespucci himself.[14] On 9 April 1495 Their Most Catholic Majesties appoint Berardi to fit out and arm twelve caravels for the restocking of Española (the fleet will later be sunk). He dies, however, on 15 December in Seville, naming Vespucci as his heir and the executor of his will. Thus the partnership of Berardi-Columbus-Vespucci is dissolved. The last of these, still in Seville in May 1499, turns power of attorney over to María Cerezo, whom he may not yet have wed. Between the end of 1500 and the beginning of 1501, he leaves Spain and heads for Lisbon, where he returns in July 1502 (or at the end of his first Portuguese voyage). But at the beginning of October, disheartened by the ingratitude of the King of Portugal, he prepares to return to Seville.

Columbus, on 5 February 1505, in a letter to his son Diego, refers to an encounter with Vespucci, who has meanwhile been summoned to Barcelona, where the Royal Court has reassembled, to answer its queries about navigation: Vespucci, bearer of the letter, "has always desired to favor me. He is a worthy person. Fate has thwarted him as it has many others: his exertions have not brought him all that reason might wish [. . .]; he is determined to do for me [before the Crown] all that he can." In fact this is the first certain testimony of his return to Seville, after the interval in Portugal (in the same year Vespucci will be naturalized as a Spanish citizen).

On 23 August 1506 the Crown orders the officials of the Casa de Contratación to oversee the rapid armament of the fleet that is to set sail, with Vespucci, for the Land of Spices (a voyage perhaps never undertaken). Then on 19 June and 16 July two

---

14 For the portion of Vespucci's life spent in Seville, the fundamental contribution is still C. Varela, 1988.

dispatches arrive from Francesco Corner to the Venetian Seigneury. The first states that Amerigo Vespucci and Juan de la Cosa have received 19,000 ducats from the Crown as reimbursement for "the acquisition of newly discovered islands, which they call terra firma" (allusion to the plan for a new voyage, on which Vespucci was to have participated as shipowner). In the second dispatch, the Venetian ambassador tells of having learned directly from Vespucci of the plan for a new voyage (possibly the same one mentioned in the preceding dispatch), for which the Florentine is said to have received 13,000 ducats; Vespucci was about to depart for Biscay, to fit out a fleet that will take him to the lands the Portuguese have discovered.

On 22 March 1508, Vespucci receives a post (created expressly for him) as "piloto mayor," with an annual income of 50,000 maravedís, plus another 25,000 for reimbursement of expenses, and on 6 August comes his official appointment, attesting to Amerigo's expertise in "determining latitude with quadrant and astrolabe." His responsibilities include teaching and examining, in the Casa de Contratación, the "pilots" of the Kingdom destined to make ocean voyages, together with the task of drawing up the general, official map ("padrón real") of the newly discovered lands, and of constantly updating them on the basis of the accounts which these same "pilots" are obliged to furnish Vespucci and the officials of the Casa. Instruction is private, given in the navigator's own house in Seville.

Vespucci dies in Seville on 22 February 1512. In his will (later revoked), dictated 9 April 1511 and rediscovered only in 1986,[15] he asks to be buried, in a Franciscan habit, in Seville's church of

15 C. Varela, "El testamento de Amerigo Vespucci," *Historiografía y bibliografía americanistas,* XXX, 1986, 2, pp. 1-18 (with facsimile), later in Varela 1988, pp. 70 ff.

San Miguel (destroyed by a fire at the beginning of this century) or in the church of the San Francisco monastery, and he names as the executors of his will the Florentine Piero Rondinelli (Berardi's successor as agent of the Medici Bank) and the Genoese Manuel Cataño (Cattani), a canon at Seville Cathedral; he leaves his possessions to his mother in Italy (he is unaware of her death) and to his brothers Antonio and Bernardo, declaring a debt of 70 ducats. He remembers the parish of Ognissanti, and asks that a requiem mass be celebrated there and thirty-three regular masses be said for his soul. By a royal decree of 28 March 1512, his widow receives a life annuity of 10,000 maravedís per year, to be deducted from the salary of Juan de Solís, the new "piloto mayor"; on María's death, the annuity is to be transferred to her sister Caterina. On 8 September, Giovanni Vespucci, Amerigo's nephew, who has been willed his "instruments" and "books," is appointed "piloto real," with an annual income of 20,000 maravedís; later, in 1525, he will be dismissed, implicated in acts of espionage for the Medici.

NOTE ON THE TEXT

An annotated critical edition of all the Italian-language letters attributed to Vespucci has been recently published by the present editor (see Formisano 1985). The same edition has been the source for the selections in two recent anthologies on the age of exploration: Einaudi's *Nuovo Mondo [The New World]* (the first Familiar Letter and the Letter to Piero Soderini) and Ricciardi's *Scopritori e viaggiatori del Cinquecento [Explorers and Travelers of the Sixteenth Century]* (the three Familiar Letters).[16] This edition is now also the basis for the English translation published here for

16 Cf. Collo and Crovetto 1991 and Pozzi 1991, respectively.

the first time. In addition to the vernacular letters the translation includes the Latin *Mundus Novus*, which, in the absence of a critical edition, is based on the text provided by Guglielmo Berchet (*Raccolta*, III, II, pp. 123-35).[17] In the present translation this text follows the Ridolfi Fragment, since the Latin guise in which it has come down to us was clearly not the work of Vespucci. It should also be noted that Pozzi's 1984 Vespucci anthology was a critically updated reediting of the eighteenth- to nineteenth-century Italian vulgate, which thus necessarily excluded the Ridolfi Fragment, as well as the second Familiar Letter (what does appear, however, is the *Mundus Novus*, preceded by the Italian *Sommario* [Abridgement] of Giovanni Battista Ramusio.)[18]

The commentary is devoted to explaining the letters' 'noteworthy' contents, drawing particular attention to the relation to other surviving travel literature, but avoiding pointing out the many textual parallels within the *corpus*. In particular, Columbus's writings (chiefly the *Diario de a bordo* and the letter of 1493 to Sánchez [referred to as *Carta*]) are cited in the Consuelo Varela edition of Cristóbal Colón, *Textos*, 1984.

The translation faithfully reproduces the original text, directly transliterating in modern form the identifiable place-names.

---

17 For an examination of the textual tradition, cf. Sarnow and Trubenbach 1903. A list of editions is provided by Hirsch 1976.

18 Cf. Ramusio, I., pp. 670-681: *Sommario di Amerigo Vespucci fiorentino, di due sue navigazioni, al magnifico M. Pietro Soderini, gonfalonier della magnifica republica di Firenze*. We should not forget that Ramusio made direct additions in the text, padding it with a series of learned allusions that appear neither in the Latin version nor in the Venetian vernacular version of the *Paesi novamente retrovati [Newly Discovered Lands]*, and, as far as the Soderini letter is concerned, combining it with the account of the second and third voyage the *Lettera* gives (cf. ibid., pp. 659-669).

The Appendices are taken from Markham 1894 (minus the notes that have been superseded by later Vespucci scholarship), except for Appendix D, which is from Waldseemüller 1907. Each text is preceded by a brief introduction.

CHRONOLOGY

1452 (or 1454)   Born in Florence on March 9

1470-80   To Paris on a diplomatic mission. Back to Florence, enters the service of Lorenzo di Pierfrancesco de' Medici as administrator.

1492-95   In Seville on behalf of Lorenzo, Vespucci engages in commerce and banking. He later joins Columbus and Giannotto Berardi's trade company.

1497-98   First voyage. From Spain, to Venezuela and Haiti.

1499-1500   Second voyage. From Spain, to Cape Verde, Venezuela and Brazil.

1501-2   Third voyage. From Portugal, to Brazil and Patagonia; return by way of Sierra Leone.

1503-4   Fourth voyage. From Portugal, to Brazil.

1505   Back to Seville. Bestowed Spanish citizenship.

1508   Appointed "Pilot Major" by the King of Spain.

1512   Dies in Seville on February 22.

THE LETTERS OF
AMERIGO VESPUCCI

LETTER I

TO LORENZO DI PIERFRANCESCO DE' MEDICI

Copy of a letter written by Amerigo Vespucci from Cadiz,
upon their return from the isles of India; and first:[1]

My Magnificent Lord: Much time has passed since I last wrote
to Your Magnificence, for the mere reason that nothing of note
has happened to me. And the present letter is to give you the news
that I returned about one month ago[2] from the Indian regions,
brought safely back by the grace of God to this, the city of Seville,
· by way of the Ocean Sea, and because I believe Your Magnificence will be pleased to hear of all that took place on the voyage,
and of the most marvelous things I encountered upon it. And as I
am somewhat given to prolixity, it might best be taken up and
read when you have amplest space for it, rather like fruit after the
table has been cleared.

Your Magnificence doubtless knows how, at the commission
of their Highnesses the Sovereigns of Spain, I departed with two
caravels on 18 May 1499 to go off and make discoveries in
the western regions by way of the Ocean Sea;[3] and I set my course
along the African coast, navigating by way of the Fortunate
Islands, now called the Canary Islands. And then, when I had
secured all necessary provisions, and we had said our orisons
and prayers, we set sail from an island known as Gomera,[4] and
turning our prows to the southwest, sailed for twenty-four days
with a fresh wind, without sighting any land. After the twenty-
four days we did sight land,[5] and we found that we had sailed

3

about thirteen hundred leagues from the city of Cadiz, in a southwesterly direction. On seeing land at last we gave thanks to God, launched the boats, and with sixteen men went ashore, to a land we found so full of trees it was a great marvel—not only the size of the trees but their verdure too, for they never shed their foliage, and the sweet scent emanating from them (for all are aromatic) was so soothing to our nostrils that it had quite a restorative effect upon us. And we rowed along the shore in the boats to see if we might find any suitable place to land; and, since it was shallows, we labored into the night without finding a passage or a fit place to enter inland; we were prevented not only by its being lowland, but also by the density of the trees; so that we decided to return to the ships, and to go further on and try landing elsewhere. And we saw something marvelous in that sea: fifteen leagues from land, we found the water as fresh as a river,[6] and drank from it, filling all our empty casks.

And upon our return to the vessels, we weighed anchor and set sail, turning our prows southward, since it was my intention to see whether I could round a cape of land which Ptolemy calls the Cape of Cattigara, which is near the Sinus Magnus;[7] for in my opinion it was not far from there, to judge by the degrees of longitude and latitude (which will be stated hereafter).

Sailing southward along the coast, we saw two very large *ríos*, or rivers, issuing out of that land, one running from west to east, some four leagues (or sixteen miles) wide; the other, running from south to north, three leagues wide;[8] and I believe it was these two rivers which caused the sea water to be fresh, given their size. And seeing that the coast was consistently lowland, we determined to enter one of the rivers with our boats, and to continue up it until we found some suitable spot to land or some inhabited point. And having readied our boats, laden with four days' provisions, we embarked on the river with twenty well-armed men. We navigated this river with oars fifteen leagues in nearly two days, attempting to land at many points.[9] Wherever we paused, we continually found the land to be continuous lowland, and so thick with trees that a bird could barely fly through it. And thus navigating over the river, we saw quite definite signs that the interior land was inhabited; and because the caravels were still resting in a dangerous spot should any crosswind arise, after two full days we thus decided to return to them.

What I and my men saw there was an infinite number of birds of various forms and colors, and so many parrots, of such diverse kinds, that it was a marvel: some red like cochineal, others green and red and lemon-yellow, still others solid green or black and flesh-colored; and the song of the other birds in the trees was a thing so fair, and so melodious, that many times we halted, seized by their sweetness. The trees there are so beautiful and fragrant, that we thought perhaps we had entered the Earthly Paradise; and not one of those trees, nor their fruits, were like our own. In the river we saw many different varieties of fish.

Having reached the ships, we raised anchor and set sail, turning our prows continually southward. And sailing on this course, at about forty leagues out to sea, we met with a sea current running southeast to northwest,[10] so great and flowing so furiously, that we were taken with great fear, and put in grave danger: the current made those of the Strait of Gibraltar or of the Faro of Messina[11] seem like stagnant pools in comparison; so strong was it that once it met our prow, we could gain no headway, even though we had a fresh wind before us. Given the little progress we were making and the great danger of our situation, we decided to turn our prows northwest, and sail northward. And since, if I remember correctly, Your Magnificence understands something of cosmography, I want to describe our position to you in longitude and latitude.

I tell you that we sailed so far south that we entered the Torrid Zone, and went within the Tropic of Cancer. You can be sure that within a few days of sailing through the Torrid Zone, we sighted four shadows of the sun, and when the sun appeared to us and its midday zenith—that is, the sun being in our meridian—we had no shadow at all: many times I pointed this out to the entire company, so that they could bear witness to this fact for the sake of the common people, who are ignorant of how the solar sphere moves through its zodiacal circle; for I once saw the shadow to the south, and another time to the north, and yet another time to the west, and another to the east, and sometimes for an hour or two in the course of the day we had no shadow. And we sailed so far south through the Torrid Zone that we found ourselves beneath the equator, with both the poles at the edge of the horizon; and we moved six degrees[12] beyond it, and completely lost sight of the North Star, and the very stars of Ursa Minor, or more precisely, the Guards which revolve around the firmament,[13] were scarcely to be seen. And as I longed to be the author who would designate the other polar star of the firmament, I lost the sleep of many a night contemplating the movement of the stars of the other pole, in order to determine which of them moved less, and was nearest the firmament; and yet I could not, for all the bad nights I had, and the many instruments I used—among them quadrant and astrolabe—mark a star that moved less than ten degrees around the firmament; so that I remained unsatisfied within myself at designating any the South Pole, because of the great circle they made around the firmament. And while pursuing this, I recalled a passage from our poet Dante from the first canto of *Purgatorio*, when he imagines he is leaving

6

this hemisphere in journeying to the other. Wishing to describe
the South Pole, he says:

> Then I turned to the right, setting my mind
> upon the other pole, and saw four stars
> not seen before except by the first people.
> Heaven appeared to revel in their flames:
> o northern hemisphere, because you were
> denied that sight, you are a widower![14]

It seems to me that in these verses the Poet seeks to describe by
the "four stars" the pole of the other firmament, and even now I
have no doubt that what he says is true: for I noted four stars[15]
forming the figure of an almond, and moving little; and should
God grant me life and health, I hope to return to that hemisphere
soon, not leaving it until I have observed the pole. I would say, in
conclusion, that we sailed so far south that our course reached
60½ degrees[16] from the latitude of the city of Cadiz, because
above that city the pole rises 35½ degrees, and we went six
degrees beyond the equator. Let this suffice concerning latitude.
Yet you must note that we were sailing in the months of July,
August, and September, when, as you know, the sun reigns
longest in our own hemisphere, describing a larger arc by day and
a smaller one by night: while we were at the equator, or within
four to six degrees of it—which was during July and August—the
difference between day and night was imperceptible, day and
night being almost equally long, or in any case scarcely different.
  As for longitude, I would say that it was so hard for me to
determine it that I had great trouble even knowing with certainty
what course I had taken in longitude; and so hard did I labor at
this that finally I found no better solution than to keep vigil

through the night, watching the opposition of one planet to another, in particular of the moon with the other planets, because the planet of the moon has a course swifter than that of any other; and I compared this against the *Almanac* of Regiomontanus,[17] composed for the meridian of the city of Ferrara, and verified it against the calculations of the *Tables* of King Don Alfonso.[18] And after many nights' watching, on the night of 23 August 1499, there was a conjunction of the moon with Mars, which, according to the *Almanac*, was to occur at midnight or half an hour before. I found that, when the moon rose on our horizon, an hour and a half after the sun had set, the planet had passed into the east, which is to say that the moon was about a degree and some minutes to the east of Mars, and at midnight was five and a half degrees to the east, more or less.[19] Thus, setting up the proportion: "If twenty-four hours equal 360 degrees, what do 5½ hours equal?", I find the answer to be 82½ degrees;[20] and such was my longitude from the meridian of Cadiz. For, giving 16⅔ leagues to every degree, I reckoned that we were 1,366⅔ leagues (or 5,466⅔ miles) west of Cadiz. And I give 16⅔ leagues to each degree because, according to Ptolemy and Alfraganus,[21] the earth rotates 24,000 miles, or 6000 leagues: which, divided by 360 degrees, makes each degree equal 16⅔ leagues. I verified this calculation many times with the pilots' charting, and found it to be sound and true.

It appears to me, then, most Magnificent Lorenzo, that by this voyage of mine most philosophers who maintain that one cannot live within the Torrid Zone because of its great heat are confuted; indeed, on my voyage I have found the contrary to be true: the air is fresher and more temperate in that region than outside it, and so many people live within it that they outnumber those outside it, for a reason I shall state below, which is most certain proof that practice is of greater worth than theory.

Thus far I have related how far to the south and west I sailed; it remains now for me to tell you about the state of the land we found and the nature of the inhabitants and their customs, and the animals we saw, and many other things met with that are worthy of record. Let me say that after our journey had turned northward, the first land we found to be inhabited was an island ten degrees from the equator;[22] and when we were near it we saw a host of people on the shore looking at us as though at something wondrous. We anchored about a mile from the land, equipped the boats and went ashore with twenty-two well-armed men; and when the people saw us land and saw that we were different from them in nature, since they are beardless, and men and women alike wear no clothing at all, exactly as they were emerging from their mothers' wombs, so they go about, not covering their shame; and so too with the difference in color, for we are white, and they grayish or tawny like lions; so that being fearful of us, they all fled into the woods, and it was with great effort, by means of signs, that we reassured them and associated with them. And we discovered that they were of a race called Cannibals, for almost the majority of this race, if not all, live off human flesh: and of this fact Your Magnificence can be certain. They do not eat one another, but navigate in certain vessels of theirs, called canoes, and they go to neighboring islands or lands in search of prey from among the races that are either their enemies or different from them; and they do not eat females, but rather keep them as slaves.[23] And this we verified in the many regions where we found such people, for many times we saw the bones and heads of some of those they had eaten, nor do they deny it, and their enemies also told us of them, living as they do in continual fear of them. These are people of quite courteous disposition, and fine stature; they go about completely naked. Their weapons are bows and arrows—which they carry with them—and round shields; they are very valiant and energetic people; they are excellent archers. In the end we did converse with them, and they took us to a village of theirs inland about two leagues, and they gave us a meal; and whatever was asked of them, they gave at once, though more out of fear than of love, I think. And after an entire day with them, we returned to our vessels, still remaining on friendly terms with them.

We sailed along the coast of this island and saw a large village by the shore. We took our boats to land, and found them waiting for us there, all of them laden with their provisions, and they gave us a fine meal of their customary food. And seeing that they were such good people, and dealt so well with us, we could not think to take anything from them; we set sail and arrived at a gulf called the Gulf of Paria, and we prepared to anchor before a very large river which causes the water in this gulf to be fresh;[24] and we saw a large village standing beside the sea which had so many people in it that it was a marvel, and all of them were unarmed. And with a sign of peace we went ashore in the boats; and they received us with great love and took us to their houses, where they prepared a fine meal. Here they gave us three kinds of wine to drink, not of the vine but, like beer, made from fruits,[25] and very good it was. Here we ate many fresh myrobalans,[26] a most regal fruit, and they gave us many other fruits as well, none like our own, and very savory, all aromatic in taste and fragrance. They gave us some small pearls and eleven large ones, and told us through signs that if we wished to wait a few days, they would go and fish for them and bring us many more: but we did not care to linger there. They gave us many parrots of various colors, and we parted as fine friends. These people informed us that those from the aforementioned island were Cannibals, and told us how they ate human flesh.

We emerged from this gulf and sailed along the land, all the while finding it greatly populated; and when we found the opportunity, we would deal with them, and they gave us what they had, and all we asked of them. They all go about naked as they were born, without the least shame: yet to relate in full what little shame they have would mean broaching improper matters; better to be silent about it. After having sailed about four hundred leagues, continually along the coast, we concluded that this was continental land—which I esteem to be bounded by the eastern part of Asia, this being the beginning of its western part—for many times we chanced to see various animals, such as lions,[27] deer, roe deer, boars, rabbits and other land animals not found in islands, but only on mainland. Exploring about the interior one day with twenty men, we saw a snake, or serpent, some eight braccia long,[28] and the width of my waist: it frightened us very much, and at the sight of it we returned to the sea. Many times I saw the most ferocious animals and large snakes.

And sailing along the coast, each day we discovered an infinite number of people and various languages until, having sailed four hundred leagues along the coast, we began to encounter people who did not want our friendship, but stood in wait for us with their weapons, which are bows and arrows, and other weapons they have. And when we went ashore in the boats, they prevented our landing, so that we were forced to fight with them; and by the end of the battle they had fared badly at our hands, for, as they always go naked, we made a great slaughter of them: for it befell us many times that sixteen of us would fight against two thousand of them, and in the end we would put them to rout, and kill many, and pillage their houses. And one day in particular, we saw a great number, all armed and arrayed to stave us our landing. We heavily armed twenty-six of our men and covered the boats because of the arrows they were shooting at us,[29] which even before we landed were wounding some of our crew. They held us off as long as they could, but finally we landed and fought most furiously with them: and the reason they persisted against us with such spirit and courage was that they did not know what sort of weapon a sword was, nor how it cuts. And fighting thus, so great was the host of people that charged upon us, so great the multitude of arrows, that we could not withstand this; and having all but abandoned the hope of living, we turned about to head back to the boats. And thus fleeing in retreat, one of our sailors, a Portuguese man fifty-five years old, who had stayed guarding the boat, seeing the danger we were in, leapt ashore from it, and shouted loudly, "Face your enemy now, boys, for God will give you victory!" And he flung himself down on his knees and offered a prayer; and then launched a great assault upon the Indians, together with all the rest of us, wounded though we were, so that the Indians turned their backs to us, and started fleeing; and in the end we routed them and killed 150 of them, and set fire to 180 of their houses.[30] And since we were badly wounded and exhausted, we returned to the vessels, and repaired to a harbor, where we remained for twenty days, only in order for the doctor to treat us: and we all pulled through but for one who was wounded in the left breast. And once we had recovered, we sailed on; and along the same coast we had occasion many times to fight with innumerable people, and were always victorious over them.

And sailing on in this way, we approached an island fifteen leagues from the mainland;[31] and since upon arriving we saw no people, we determined to go and explore it. Eleven men went ashore, and found a path, and we set about to follow it 2½ leagues inland; and we found a village of twelve houses, where we found only seven females, of such large stature that not one of them was not a span and a half taller than I. And when they saw us, they were much afraid of us, and the chief one among them, who most certainly was a woman of good judgment, led us by signs to a house, and had refreshment given to us. And we, on seeing such large women, decided to steal two of them, young ones fifteen years of age, to make a present of them to the Sovereigns, for they were beyond all doubt creatures of far greater stature than common men. And while we were discussing this plan, thirty-six men came and entered the house where we were drinking; and they were of such tall stature, that each one of them was taller kneeling than I am standing: in sum, they were of the stature of giants, the size and proportion of their bodies corresponding to their height, for each of the women seemed a Penthesilea, and all the men Antaei.[32] And when they entered, some of us were taken with such fear that to this day they do not feel safe. They carried bows and arrows and huge clubs fashioned like swords, and, when they saw our small stature, they started to speak with us in order to find out who we were, and from what region we came; and we, doing all we could to keep peace, answered them by signs that we were men of peace, going about to see the world. In the end we thought it wise to depart from them without asking questions in return and we took the same path by which we came, and they accompanied us as far as the sea, until we boarded our vessels. The great majority of trees on this island are of brazilwood, and as good as that of the Levant.

From this island we went to a neighboring one ten leagues off, and found a very large village, where they had houses built with great skill upon the sea, as in Venice;[33] and wondering at such a thing, we decided to go to see them, and, when we reached their houses, they sought to prevent our entering them. They discovered then how swords cut, and thought it best to let us enter; and we found that they kept their houses full of very fine cotton wool, and all the beams of their houses were of brazilwood; and we took quite a lot of cotton and brazilwood, and headed back to the vessels. You should know that everywhere we landed, we found great abundance of cotton wool and fields full of cotton plants, enough for all the caracks[34] and vessels in the world to be laden with the cotton and brazilwood of those regions.

At length we sailed along the coast another 300 leagues, always encountering savage people, and innumerable times we fought with them, and captured some twenty of them, among whom were speakers of seven mutually incomprehensible languages: it is maintained that there are only seventy-seven languages in the world,[35] but I say that there are more than one thousand, for those alone which I have heard number more than forty.

After having sailed along this land seven hundred leagues or more, apart from the countless islands we had seen, the vessels suffered much wear and were taking in such an endless amount of water, that they could barely remedy this with two bailing pumps, and the men were very weary and oppressed, and food provisions lacking, as we found ourselves, according to the pilot's chart, near an island called Española—the very one that Admiral Columbus discovered six years ago[36]—120 leagues away, we decided to go to it, and there, since it is inhabited by Christians, we would mend our vessels and give our crew rest and get provisions, since between this island and Castile[37] lie thirteen hundred leagues of sea, and not a single intervening stretch of land. And in seven days we reached this island, where we stayed some two months, and refitted the ships and obtained our provisions; and we decided to go to the northern region, where we found countless people and discovered more than a thousand islands, most of them inhabited, and the people again naked, ever fearful and of feeble mind, and we did with them whatever we wished.

This last region we discovered was very dangerous for us to navigate because of the shallows and low sea we found there; for many times we came close to foundering. We sailed two hundred leagues directly north on this sea; and the men were already weary and exhausted from having been at sea for nearly a year, with an allowance of only six ounces of bread and three small measures of water a day; and since it was dangerous to keep the vessels longer at sea, the men remonstrated, saying that they wanted to return to Castile, to their homes, and no longer wanted to tempt the sea and fortune. For that reason we resolved to capture slaves, load the vessels with them, and head toward Spain. And we were on certain islands[38] and took 232 souls by force, loaded them on, and headed for Castile. And in 67 days we crossed the ocean and reached the islands of the Azores, which belong to the king of Portugal and are at a distance of 300 leagues from Cadiz. Once we had restored ourselves there, we sailed on to Castile; but the wind was against us, and we were forced to go to the Canary Islands, and from the Canaries to the isle of Madeira, and from Madeira to Cadiz. We were thirteen months on this voyage, encountering great dangers and discovering endless Asian land and a great many islands, most of which are inhabited: for, to judge by the many times I calculated with compass, we sailed some five thousand leagues.

In conclusion, we passed the equator by 6½ degrees, and later returned to the north far enough for the North Star to rise above our horizon 35½ degrees;[39] and to the west, we sailed 84 degrees from the meridian of the city and port of Cadiz. We discovered boundless land, we saw quite a truly infinite number of people, speaking various tongues, and all naked. On that land we saw many wild animals and different kinds of birds, and a countless variety of trees, all very fragrant. We brought back pearls and gold in its nascent or crude state. We brought back two stones, one the color of emerald, the other of amethyst, both very hard and half a span long and three fingers wide: these Sovereigns esteem them highly, and have placed them among their treasured jewels. We brought back a large piece of crystal which some jewelers say is beryl, and according to what the Indians told us, they have it in abundance. We brought back fourteen pearls the color of flesh which greatly pleased the queen, and many other gems that seemed beautiful to us. We did not bring back a great quantity of these things, since we did not stay long in any place but were always sailing on. On arriving in Cadiz we sold our slaves, of which we had two hundred, the others among the initial 232 having died on the ocean. And when all the damages inflicted on the vessels were deducted, five hundred ducats remained, which had to be divided into fifty-five shares, so that only a little went to each man; and yet we were pleased to be alive, and rendered our thanks to God, for in the entire voyage, out of the fifty-seven Christian men aboard, only two had died, killed by Indians. Since my return I have twice had quartan agues, but trust in God to be well again soon, because they do not last long, and come without chills. I have passed over many things worthy of record lest I grow more prolix than I am; they are preserved for the pen and in memory. Here they are fitting up three vessels for me, so that I may again go forth to make discoveries, and I think these will be ready by mid-September.[40] May it please Our Lord to give me health and a good voyage, for I hope both to bring back very great news and to discover the island of Taprobane,[41] which lies between the Indian Ocean and Ganges Sea;[42] after which I intend to return to my homeland and finish out the days of my old age in repose.

For the present I shall not enlarge my discourse, for many things remain to be written of, from a failure to recall everything, and in order not to be more prolix than I have been.

I have resolved, Magnificent Lorenzo, that, just as I have given you an account by letter of what happened to me, I shall send you two depictions of the world, made and ordered by my own hand and knowledge: one chart will be a flat rendering and the other a map of the world in spherical form, which I intend to send to you by sea with one Francesco Lotti, himself a Florentine who is here now. I believe they will be to your liking, especially the globe; for, not long ago, I made one for their Highnesses the Sovereigns, and they prize it highly. It was my intention to come with them personally, but the new departure to set out once more on discoveries leaves me neither room nor time. There is no lack in your city of those who know how the world is depicted, and some perhaps may wish to emend something in what I have done; nonetheless let him who would emend me wait for my coming, as it may be that I shall defend myself.

I trust Your Magnificence will have heard the news brought by the fleet sent by the King of Portugal[43] two years ago to make discoveries about the region of Guinea:[44] such a voyage as that I do not call discovery, but merely a going to discovered lands, since, as you will see by the map, they navigate continually in sight of land, and sail along the entire southern part of Africa, which is to proceed upon a way discussed by all the authorities in cosmography. It is true that the navigation has been most profitable, which these days is what counts most, and especially in this kingdom, where inordinate greed reigns out of all order. I hear that they passed beyond the Red Sea, and reached the Persian

Gulf, and a city called Calicut, which is situated between the Persian Gulf and the river Indus;[45] and now the King of Portugal has once more equipped twelve ships at very great expense,[46] and has sent them to those parts, and surely they will accomplish great things, if they return safely.

Today is 18 July 1500,[47] and there is nothing else to report. May our Lord preserve and increase the exalted state of Your Most Serene Magnificence, as desires

Your Magnificence's

humble servant Amerigo Vespucci

LETTER II

*Copy of a letter written by Amerigo Vespucci from the island
of Cape Verde in the Ocean Sea to Lorenzo di
Pierfrancesco de' Medici 4 June 1501.*

My Magnificent Patron: 8 May was the last time I wrote to
you,[1] from Lisbon, where I stood ready to embark upon this
present voyage which now, with the help of the Holy Spirit, I have
begun; and, having supposed that I would not be able to write to
you until my return, it seems that chance has given me the
opportunity to write to you not only from distant lands, but from
high seas as well.

You will have heard, Lorenzo, either through my letter or
through that of our fellow Florentines in Lisbon, that while
staying in Seville I was summoned by the King of Portugal,[2] and
that he asked me to prepare to enter his service on this voyage, in
which I embarked at Lisbon on the thirteenth of last month,[3] and
we took our course southward, and sailed until we passed within
sight of the Fortunate Islands, now called the Canary Islands, and
we passed them at a distance, holding our course along the
African coast. And we sailed on until we arrived here, at a cape
called Cape Verde, which is the beginning of the province of
Ethiopia,[4] and lies on the same meridian as the Fortunate Islands,
namely, at fourteen degrees from the equator;[5] where by chance
we found two ships of the King of Portugal anchored on their
return from the eastern regions of India, they being among the

ones which went to Calicut fourteen months ago[6]—when there were thirteen vessels—and with them I have had very lengthy conversations, not so much about their voyage as about the coast of the land along which they had run, and the riches they found there, and what the inhabitants have. All will be mentioned briefly in this letter to Your Magnificence: not by way of cosmography, since the fleet had neither a cosmographer nor a mathematician in its company (which was a great error), but it will be recounted as confusedly as they reported it to me, except that I have somewhat corrected it with the *Cosmography* of Ptolemy.

The fleet of the King of Portugal departed from Lisbon in 1499, in the month of April,[7] and they sailed southward to the isles of Cape Verde, which lie approximately fourteen degrees from the equator and beyond all meridians to the west,[8] so that you could say that they lie six degrees further west than the Canary Islands, more or less: for you well know that Ptolemy and most schools of cosmography locate the end of the inhabited west at the Fortunate Islands, which, by astrolabe and quadrant, lie at the latitude of [. . .]; and so I have found it to be. Longitude is a more difficult matter, for it has been made known to few, and then almost solely to those who keep vigil and observe the conjunction of the moon with the planets: to determine the said longitude, I have lost many nights of sleep and have shortened my life by ten years; and I count this all as time well spent, for I hope to be famous for many an age, if I return safe and sound from this voyage: may God not deem this pride, for all my labor is dedicated to His holy service.

I return now to my subject. As I have said, those thirteen aforementioned vessels sailed south from the Cape Verde Islands with a wind said to be between south and southwest,[9] and after having sailed about seven hundred leagues in twenty days—each league 4½ miles[10]—they came to a land where there lived a white and naked people—the very same land which I discovered for the Sovereigns of Castile, but that it lies farther to the east[11]—I wrote to you of it in another letter—where they say they purchased all the fresh supplies they required.

And they departed thence[12] and sailed eastward, on a course southeast by east. And when they were far from that land, they met with so turbulent a sea and such great gusts of wind blowing to the southwest that it capsized five of their ships[13] and submerged them in the sea with all their crews aboard—would that God had mercy on their souls—and they say that other eight ships[14] ran their course with bare masts, that is, without sails, for forty-eight days and nights in sorest distress. They ran on so far that they found themselves windward of the Cape of Good Hope, which is to be found along the coast of Ethiopia, ten degrees south of the Tropic of Capricorn: I say that it lies thirty-three degrees south of the equator; so that, establishing the proportion of the parallel, we find that cape to have a longitude in the inhabited west of sixty-two degrees, more or less: which is to say on the meridian of Alexandria.[15]

And from here they then sailed north by northeast, sailing continually along the coast, which, in my opinion, is the beginning of Asia and the province of Arabia Felix, which is the land of Prester John,[16] since there they had news of the Nile, which lay to the west of them: for as you know, this river divides Africa from Asia.[17] And on this coast they saw countless people and cities, and at some of these put into port; and the first was Sofala which they say is a city as big as Cairo, and has a gold mine, and they say that they pay a tribute to their king of two hundred thousand gold *miticalli* every year, every *miticale* being worth approximately a gold *castellana*.[18] And from there they departed and came to

Mozambique, where there is said to be a great deal of aloe and boundless gum-lac and much silk cloth, and as large a population as that of Cairo. And from Mozambique they went to Kilwa and Mombasa, and from Mombasa to Dimodaza and Malindi, then to Mogadishu and Camperaia, Zendach, then to Amaal, and then to Dabul and Albacaron: and all these cities are on the coast of the Ocean Sea and reach as far as the strait of the Red Sea; which you should know is not red, but is like our own, and only has the name 'Red.'[19] And all these cities are extremely rich in gold and jewels and textiles and spices and drugs, which are not all native to them, but are brought in wagons from the regions of India, as you can picture to yourself, for otherwise it would be long to relate.

From Albacaron, and across the strait of the Red Sea, they go to Mecca, where a ship in this newly arrived fleet visited.[20] And to this point I have written about the coast of Arabia Felix; now I shall tell you of the coast of the Red Sea toward India, that is, within the strait of that sea.

At the mouth of the strait there is a port on the Red Sea which is called Aden, where stands a great city; further to the north there is another port, called Camaram and Ansuva; then there is another port called Hudaydah; then from Hudaydah one goes on to Lamoin, and from Lamoin to Jiddah. This port Jiddah is near Mount Sinai, which, as you know, is in Arabia Deserta, which is said to be the stopping place for all vessels that travel from India and from Mecca; and it is said that in this port they unload all the spices and drugs and jewels and leave everything there; after which the caravans of camels come from Cairo and Alexandria, and bring those goods back with them, over the desert of Arabia, this journey said to be eighty leagues. And they say they do not navigate on this Red Sea except by day, because of the many rocks and shoals it contains; and many other things were told me about this sea which I do not mention here, lest I grow prolix.

Now I shall tell of the coast of the Red Sea on the African side. At the mouth of the strait of that sea lies Zeila, the lord of which city is a Moor named Agi d'Arabi, and they say the place is three days distant from the port of Jiddah; it possesses much gold, many elephants, and infinite stores of goods.

From Zeila to Darbarui: Prester John is lord of the land between these two ports and Darboiam Azala; and opposite them is a port named Tui, which belongs to the great Sultan of Babylon;[21] after Tui comes Edem and after Edem, Zeon. This is as much as I could learn of the Red Sea: I defer to any who knows it better.

I have yet to say what I heard of the coast of Mecca within the Persian Sea, which was the following.

Leaving from Mecca along the seacoast one comes to a city which is called Hormuz, which is a port at the mouth of the Persian Sea; and then from Hormuz one goes to Tuns, and from Tuns to Tunas, then to Capan, then to Lecor, then to Dua, then to Torfsis, then to Pares, then to Scucan, then to Tatar. All these ports, which are heavily populated, are set within the coastline of the Persian Sea: I believe that I shall encounter many more when I reach that area, for in truth I refer to what a man worthy of trust named Gaspar[22] told me, who had travelled from Cairo as far as a province named Malacca, which is situated on the coast of the Indian Sea (I believe this to be the province which Ptolemy calls Gedrosia).[23] They say that this Persian Sea is very rich, but one must not believe everything one hears, and thus I leave that to the pen of one who will better provide the truth.

Now I have yet to speak of the coast that stretches from the strait of the Persian Sea toward the Indian Sea, according to what many tell me who were in that fleet, and especially the said Gaspar, who knows many languages and the names of many provinces and cities: as I say, he is a very trustworthy man, because he has twice made the voyage from Portugal to the Indian Sea.[24]

From the mouth of the Persian Sea one sails to a city called Zabul, and from Zabul to Goga, and from Goga to Zedeuba, and on to Nui, then Bacanur, then Salur, then Mangalore, then Bhatkal, then Calnur, then Dharmadam, then Panthalayini Killam, then Edakkad, then Calicut (this city is very big, and the Portuguese fleet rested in it);[25] then from Calicut to Belfur, then to Scailat, then Rajahmundry, then Parappanagadi, then Tanur, then Propornat, then Cuninam, then Lonam, then Belingut, then Palur, then Kodangolor, then Cochin, then Kayankulam, then Teinquolon, then Cain, then Coroncaram, then Scomondel, then Negapatam, then Delmatan, then Kharepatam, then Conimat: this is as far as the Portuguese fleet has sailed, and if no one reports the latitude and longitude of that voyage, it is because it would have been impossible for any but a very experienced mariner to establish them. And I hope in this voyage of mine to revisit and traverse much of the aforementioned area, and to discover much more; and upon my return I shall give a full and true report of everything. May the Holy Spirit go with me.

That Gaspar who told me the aforesaid things—and many Christians, having been to some of these places, confirmed them—later told me the following. He said that he had made his way into India into a kingdom called Pulicat, which is a very large kingdom rich in gold and pearls and jewels and precious stones; and told of having gone into the interior to Mailapur, Giapatan, Malacca, Tenasserim, Pegu, Scarnai, Bengala, Otezan, and Mergui. And this Mergui he says is near a big river called Emparlicat;

and this Emparlicat is a city where the body of the Apostle Saint Thomas[26] is buried, and there are many Christians there. And he told me that he had been to many islands, and in particular to one called Ceylon, which he says measures three hundred leagues in circumference, and that the sea and the river had consumed another four hundred leagues of it. He told me it was an island very rich in precious stones and pearls and spices of every sort and drugs, and other riches such as elephants and a great cavalry, so that I believe this to be the island Taprobane, judging by his description; and he further told me that he had never heard the name Taprobane mentioned in those parts, which, as you know, lies entirely in front of the river Indus.

Likewise he told me that he had been to another neighboring island called Sumatra, which is as large as Ceylon and as rich, so that if Ceylon is not Taprobane, Sumatra is.[27] Innumerable ships laden with all kinds of spices, drugs, and precious jewels leave from these two islands for Persia and Arabia. And they say they have seen a great number of ships in these parts, and that they are very large, between forty and fifty thousand cantars in capacity, and these are called 'junks,' and have the masts of very large boats, with three or four crow's nests upon each mast; the sails are made of rushes: they are not built with iron, but instead are intertwined with cord (it seems the sea is not stormy there); they have mortars, but are not swift vessels, nor do they venture far out to sea, but always sail within sight of land. It happened that this Portuguese fleet, to fulfill a request of the King of Calicut, seized a ship loaded with elephants, rice, and more than three hundred men, and a caravel of seventy tons made this capture; and on another occasion they sank twelve boats. Then they came to an island called Arabuga, and Maluca[28] and many other islands in the Indian Sea, which are the ones that Ptolemy says surround the isle of Taprobane, and they are all rich.

The said fleet is returning to Portugal; and meanwhile the eight ships[29] remaining lost a cargo of great wealth, said to be worth one hundred thousand ducats;[30] one of the five ships[31] which lost sight of the captain's ship in the tempests has arrived here today, as I have said.[32] I believe that the others will arrive safely: so may it please God.

Those ships carry the following. They are laden with infinite cinnamon, fresh and dried ginger, much pepper and cloves, nutmeg, mace, musk, civet, storax, benzoin, purslane, mastic, incense, myrrh, red and white sandalwood, lignum aloe, camphor, ambergris, much gum-lac, mummy, indigo, cadmium, opium, hepatic aloe, cassia, and many other drugs it would take too much time to recount. About the jewels I know nothing certain, except that I saw many diamonds and rubies and pearls, among which I saw a ruby in crude stone form of a most beautiful color, weighing 7 ½ carats. At the moment I cannot enlarge upon this because the vessels are [. . .] and keep me from writing; you will have news from Portugal. In conclusion, the King of Portugal enjoys very great trade and wealth: may God increase it. They believe that the spices will come from those parts to Alexandria and to Italy, according to their quality and worth; so goes the world.

Believe, Lorenzo, that what I have written thus far is the truth, and if the provinces, kingdoms, names of cities and islands in the ancient writers do not appear here, it is a sign that they have changed, as we see in our own Europe, where it is a great rarity to hear an ancient name; and for greater evidence that this is the truth, Gherardo Verde was present, who is the brother of Simon

Verde of Cadiz,[33] who travels in my company and recommends himself to you.

I see that this voyage I embark upon now is perilous to the security of our mortal existence; nonetheless I make it with a spirit resolved to serve God and the world; and if God has found use for me, He will grant me the strength he has endowed me with to carry out whatever is His will, so long as He grants eternal repose to my soul.

LETTER III

Copy of a letter from Amerigo Vespucci to Lorenzo di Pierfrancesco de' Medici, written in the year 1502 from Lisbon concerning their return'from the new lands they were sent to explore by his majesty the King of Portugal; and first:

My Magnificent Patron, Lorenzo, after due salutations, etc. When last I wrote to Your Magnificence[2] it was from the coast of Guinea, from a place called Cape Verde, by which you were informed of the start of my voyage; and by the present letter, you will be told in brief of the middle and end of it, which is what follows.

We departed from the said Cape Verde, with no initial difficulty, and equipped with all provisions, including water, firewood and other necessary supplies for sailing out upon the midst of the Ocean Sea in search of new lands; and we sailed a course southwest by south until, after sixty-four days, we reached a new land,[3] which we found to be mainland for many reasons which will be adduced in what follows. We passed by that land for about eight hundred leagues always on a southwest, ¼ west course, and we found it full of inhabitants; where I noted wondrous works of God and nature, whence I was resolved to give tidings of part of them to Your Magnificence, as I always have for my other voyages.[4]

We travelled so far upon these seas that we entered the Torrid Zone and passed south of the equator and the Tropic of Capricorn, so that the South Pole stood fifty degrees above my horizon; and my latitude from the equator was the same,[5] for we sailed nine months and twenty-seven days[6] without seeing either the Arctic Pole or Ursa Major or Minor, and conversely to the south the sight was revealed to me of countless very bright and beautiful stars, which always remain hidden in the north. There I observed the wondrous workings of their movements and their magnitudes, measuring the diameter of their orbits and notating them with geometrical figures; and many other movements of the heavens I noted down, which it would be prolix to describe: but the most remarkable of all the things I beheld on this voyage I have gathered into a small work so that, when I shall have the leisure, I may occupy myself with the task, that I may gain some fame after my death. I was intending to send you a summary of it, but this His Most Serene Highness has taken; but when he returns it to me, I shall send it. In conclusion, I was in the region of the Antipodes, on a voyage which covered a quarter of the world: the highest point of my zenith in those regions made a spherical right angle[7] with the inhabitants of the northern hemisphere, who are at a latitude of forty degrees;[8] and let that suffice.

Let us proceed to a description of the land and its inhabitants, animals, plants and other things useful and common for human life which we found in these parts.

This land is very pleasant and full of countless very large green trees, which never shed their leaves, all of them giving off the sweetest aromatic fragrances, and produce infinite kinds of fruits excellent to the taste and healthful to the body. And the fields produce many sweet and delicious herbs, flowers, and roots, and sometimes I marvelled so much at the delicate scents of the herbs and flowers, and the tastes of those fruits and roots, that I thought

I must be near the Earthly Paradise: and well I might have believed I was near it amid such things. What is there to say of the quantity of birds, and their plumes and colors and songs, and how many kinds and how beautiful they are? (I do not wish to enlarge upon this, for I doubt I would be believed); who could tell the infinite number of forest animals, the abundance of lions,[9] jaguars, catamounts—not like those in Spain but in the Antipodes—so many lynxes, baboons, monkeys of many kinds and many large snakes as well? And we saw so many other animals that I think so many kinds could not have fit into Noah's ark, so many wild boars, roe deer, deer, does, hares and rabbits; and we never once saw domestic animals.

Let us come to the rational animals. We found the entire land inhabited by people completely naked, men as well as women, without at all covering their shame. They are sturdy and well-proportioned in body, white in complexion, with long[10] black hair and little or no beard. I strove hard to understand their life and customs, since I ate and slept among them for twenty-seven days; and what I learned of them is the following.

They have no law or religious faith, they live as nature dictates, they do not know of the immortality of the soul. They have no private property among them, for they share everything. They have no borders of kingdoms or province; neither have they a king or anyone they obey: each is his own master. They do not administer justice, which is not necessary for them, since greed does not prevail among them. They live together and the houses are made like very big huts, and, for people who have no iron or any other metal, these huts or rather houses can well be called miraculous, for I have seen houses longer than 220 paces and thirty paces wide, most skillfully built; and in one of these houses five or six hundred souls may dwell. They sleep in nets of woven cotton, suspended in the air, without any covering. They eat sitting upon the ground; their food includes many roots and herbs and very good fruits, endless fish, a great abundance of shellfish, sea urchins, crabs, oysters, lobsters, shrimps, and many other foods which the sea yields. The meat they most commonly eat is human flesh, as we shall tell. When they can get it, they eat the meat of other animals and birds. But they do not catch many of them, because they have no dogs, and the land is very dense with forests which are full of ferocious beasts, and for this reason they seldom venture into the woods except in large groups.

The men are accustomed to make holes in their lips and cheeks, and in those holes they put bones or stones,[11] and you must not think they are small ones, for most of the men have no fewer than three holes (and some seven, and even nine), in which they place stone of green and white alabaster, which are half a span long and big as Catalan plums, so that they appear something utterly unnatural: they say they do this in order to appear more fierce; all in all, it is a bestial thing.

And their marriages are not with one woman, but with as many as they wish, and without much ceremony, for we have met one man who has ten women. They are jealous of their women, and if it happens that one of them should wrong the man, he punishes her by beating her and sending her away from him to live apart. They are very procreative; they have no heirs, since they have no property. When their children—that is, the female ones—are old enough to give birth, the first to deflower them must be the next closest relative after the father; and then, once thus deflowered, they are married off.

Their women observe no ceremony at childbirth, as ours do, for they eat everything; the very same day they go off to the fields to wash themselves, and they barely suffer in childbirth.

They are people who live many years, for we met many who had up to four generations of descendants, according to their recollections. And they do not know how to count days, or months or years, except that they tell time by lunar months; and when they wish to show something, and refer to time, they show it by means of stones, setting down a stone for every moon. And I found one of the oldest men who by such stone signs explained to me that he had lived seventeen hundred lunar months, which by my reckoning must be 132 years,[12] counting thirteen moons for every year.

Also they are a warlike people and very cruel to one another; and all their arms and sallies are, as Petrarch says, "entrusted to the wind,"[13] for they are bows, arrows, spears and stones; and they use no protective armor for their bodies, since they go about naked as the day they were born. Nor do they maintain any order when they make war, except that they do what their elders advise. And when they fight, they kill one another most cruelly, and the side that emerges victorious on the field buries all of their own dead, but they dismember and eat their dead enemies; and those they capture they imprison and keep as slaves in their houses: if females, they sleep with them; if males, they marry them to their daughters. And at certain times when a diabolical fury comes over them, they invite their relatives and the people to dinner, and they set them out before them—that is, the mother and all the children they have got from her—and performing certain ceremonies kill them with arrows and eat them; and they do the same to the aforesaid male slaves and the children that have come from them. And this is certain, for in their houses we found human flesh hung up for smoking, and a lot of it, and we bought ten creatures from them, both males and females, who were destined for sacrifice, or, better said, sacrilege; on this we strongly reproached them: I do not know if they will mend their ways. And what I most marvel at, given their wars and their cruelty, is that I could not learn from them why they make war upon one another: since they do not have private property, or command empires or kingdoms, and have no notion of greed, that is, greed either for things or for power, which seems to me to be the cause of wars and all acts of disorder. When we asked them to tell us the cause, the only reason they could give was that this curse had begun "in olden times," and that they wish to avenge the death of their ancestors: in sum, a bestial thing; and certainly one of their men confessed to me that he had eaten of the flesh of more than two hundred bodies; and I believe this to be true, and on this subject let this suffice.

As for the condition of the land, I should say that it is very pleasant and temperate and healthy, for in the time we spent there, which was ten months, not only did none of us die, but few were ever sick. As I have said, they live long, and do not sicken either from pestilence or corruption of the air, dying only natural deaths, unless they be suffocated by hand;[14] in conclusion, physicians would fare ill in such a place.

Since we journeyed there in the name of discovery, and with that commission departed from Lisbon, and not to seek after profit, we did not make obstacles to our exploration of the land nor seek after profit; so that we did not learn of anything useful to anyone: not because I do not think the land does not produce all kinds of riches through its excellent condition and from its parallel of the climate in which it is situated. And it is no wonder that we were not immediately made aware of all the profit to be had there, for its inhabitants prize nothing, neither gold nor silver nor other precious stones, nor anything but feathers and bones, as mentioned previously; and it is my hope that, now that his Most Serene Highness is sending voyagers there, not many years will pass before the land brings vast profit and revenue to the kingdom of Portugal.

We found there endless brazilwood, of very fine quality, enough to load all the vessels on the seas today, and it costs nothing, which is true as well of *cassiafistula*.[15] We saw crystal, and infinite scents and fragrances of spices and drugs which are not, however, known. The men tell of many miracles concerning the gold and other metals and drugs, but I am one of those like Saint Thomas: time will tell.

The heavens are generally clear, and adorned with many bright stars, all of which I noted, with their orbits.

These, in brief and only the broadest outline, are among the things I saw in those parts; many things have been left out that would be worthy of record, lest I be guilty of prolixity, and because you will find them in detail in my *Voyage*.

For the present I remain here in Lisbon, waiting for the king to decide what to do with me: may it please God that it be whatever most befits His holy service and the salvation of my soul.

LETTER IV

Copy of part of a letter by Amerigo Vespucci.

[. . .] we noticed the difference of the night growing longer and the day diminishing. In truth when we were at the latitude of fifty degrees, we were at sea and not on land, because when we managed to push off from land, we were not at an latitude greater than thirty-two degrees, and then we sailed to the southeast until we arrived at the said latitude of fifty degrees without finding land, although we judged that we were near land[1] by many visible signs, among them countless birds of various sorts and much wood in the water: most certain signs. But because the sea was very turbulent and cold, the vessels suffered much wear and the men were very weakened from having been sixteen months[2] at sea with shortage of provisions, and for many other reasons, we resolved not to go on our explorations but rather to turn back toward Portugal. And at the point where we arrived and where we turned around, we were almost sixteen hundred leagues to the south on a straight line from the city of Lisbon; for, if you set up the proportion, calculating the circumference of the earth to be twenty-four thousand miles, you will find that we had sailed about ninety-two degrees south of the city of Lisbon, which, as you can see, is more than one quarter of the terrestrial world.

As for a defense of my claim that the people in that land go about naked, this is supported by natural reason and the fact that I saw so many "that no one can enumerate them."[3] There is no merit to the argument that since you are located in the sixth climate or at the end of the fifth, how can those in the seventh who go about naked better endure the cold than we who go about in two layers of clothing? For, as the Philosopher says, "customs transform nature."[4] And surely in all my three voyages over the earth—two of which I made to the west by the Ocean Sea, following both courses of south and southwest, while on the third I took a course to the south by the Atlantic Sea—I have seen during those voyages nearly two thousand leagues of continental coast and more than five thousand islands, and many of those inhabited, and the mainland full of countless peoples, and never did I see any of them clothed, nor did they even cover more or less of their shame, men or women. And the extent of the land seen and navigated by me is contained within these two tropics, or more precisely, parallels: the one is at the northern region, thirty-three degrees from the equator, the opposite one south of that line by thirty-two degrees; and you must not think it lies within a single meridian, but rather several: because by the aforesaid calculation of latitude, I maintain that I sailed so far by land and sea that it totaled ninety-two degrees of latitude, and I have established that I travelled within different meridians, and the farthest meridian to the west was by my reckoning $5\frac{1}{3}$ hours from the meridian of this Portuguese city, and about eight hours from the meridian of Ferrara, and by hours I am speaking of the equinoctial kind.[5] Briefly to support what I assert, and to defend myself from the talk of the malicious, I maintain that I learned this by the eclipses and conjunctions of the moon with the planets; and I have lost many nights of sleep in reconciling my calculations with the precepts of those sages who have devised the manuals and written of the movements, conjunctions, aspects, and eclipses of the two luminaries and of the wandering stars, such as the wise King Don Alfonso in his *Tables,* Johannes Regiomontanus in his *Almanac,* and Blanchinus, and the Jewish rabbi Zacuto in his *Almanac,* which is perpetual; and these were composed in different meridians: King Don Alfonso's book in the meridian of Toledo, and Johannes Regiomontanus's in that of Ferrara, and the other two in that of Salamanca.[6] It is certain that I found myself, in a region that is not uninhabited but highly populated, 150 degrees west of the meridian of Alexandria, which is eight equinoctial hours. If some envious or malicious person does not believe this, let him come to me, that I may affirm this with calculations, authorities, and witnesses. And let that suffice with respect to longitude; for, if I were not so busy, I would send you full detail of all the many conjunctions which I observed, but I do not wish to become so tangled in this matter, which strikes me to be the doubt of a literary man, and not one which you have raised. Let that suffice. As for my saying that the people in that land are white, and not black, and especially those who live within the Torrid Zone, I reply to you, without transgressing the honor of philosophy, that it is not necessary that all men who live in the Torrid Zone should be black by nature, and have hot blood like the Ethiopians and the greater part of the people who live in the regions of Ethiopia;[7] for, as I have said above, I have navigated over all the parallels from Morocco to the end of Ethiopia, and passed beyond the equator thirty-two degrees to the south, and have been in many parts of Africa and Ethiopia: to the Cape of Cantin,[8] to the Cape of Anghille,[9] to Zanaga,[10] to Cape Verde, to Rio Grande, to Sierra Leone[11] which is seven degrees from the equator, and have seen and spoken with countless people, and all of them black, but more in one place than in another. And although such knowledge is the true prerogative of the philosopher, I shall not withold my opinion, be it well or ill received. I find the major cause to spring from the character of the air and the condition of the land, for the entire land of Ethiopia is very thinly populated, and there is scarcity of fresh water there, and it seldom rains, and the terrain is very sandy, and baked by the heat of the sun, and there are infinitely many sandy deserts and extremely few forests or woods, and the winds that prevail in that region are easterly ones and sciroccos, which are hot winds; and also because nature has already converted their blackness into a trait, as we see even in our regions: that the black people breed black, and if a white [. . .]¹² with a black woman, the offspring will be gray, that is, less black than the mother and less white than the father, and the converse is true as well: a sign that nature and custom work greater effects than the composition of the air and the land. Thus I conclude that, since the land and air which I have found in the same latitude as Africa and Ethiopia, or more precisely, in the same parallels, are much more pleasant and temperate and of better composition, this causes the people to be white, although they tend toward a tawny or leonine color; for, as I maintain, in those parts the air is more temperate than that of Ethiopia, and the earth much more pleasant and abundant with fresh water, and is visited almost every day by dews, and winds are northern and southern so that those parts do not have the burning heats of Ethiopia, and its land causes winds and dews which always keep the trees green and leafy; and this is certain, and let anyone who does not believe it go and see it, as I have done. There are so many woods and forests in these parts, with such huge trees, always verdant and different from ours, that it is a true wonder; and most of them yield liquors or gums and vinegars, and are of aromatic fragrance. I could expatiate upon this subject, adducing also the opposition of the sun's course or the influences of the astral bodies of the eigth sphere which reign in those parts, but shall leave such matters, to shorten the discourse, to the discretion of the wise.

As for your question you put to me about whether I passed the Tropic of Cancer with my zenith, the letter shows it, for the Tropic is twenty-three degrees and fifty-one minutes from the equator, and in fifty degrees I reached the arctic circle. Well, that was an easy question.

I have already told you how in that hemisphere the sequence of the four seasons is the very opposite of ours, since the sun's entry into the first degree of Aries, which is spring for us, for them is autumn; and when the sun is in Cancer, it is summer for us and winter for them, and so consequently with Libra and Capricorn; therefore the longest day I spent in those parts was 2 December, and the longest night 2 June. And this was noted by me countless times using many of my instruments.

You advance an argument to demonstrate that this region is cold by saying that when the sun is in the first degree of Cancer, it is farther from the line of the equator; and this is false, for as you well know, according to mathematical demonstrations, the sun has two different [. . .]¹³ in its orbit, one called the apogee and the other the perigee; and when the sun is in its apogee, it is, I think, in the third degree of Cancer, so that in this season it is farther in its line from the earth than at any other, and therefore this should cause the air to be colder, yet we see the opposite, that in that season we experience the severest heat; however, this is caused by the fact that in that season the sun comes closest to our zenith and casts its rays more perpendicularly, for which reason the dense vapors high up in the region of the air are dissipated more quickly. So, for this reason we must affirm that, as the sun stands in the first degree of Cancer, it will be in a more transverse line for those who live in the other hemisphere, and thus it will be as cold there as the sun is for us at its perigee, which is about the third degree of Capricorn, and which for us is in its greatest declination, when the most transversal rays strike us, and lack the strength to dissipate the high vapors, as happens with those of the other hemisphere. And I could give you innumerable other reasons, but let these suffice for now.

As for what you say regarding the end of the first chapter of my letter,[14] where I stated that the intersection of two lines, that is the line of my zenith and that of my parallel, made a spherical right angle for me, what I said and still say holds true; but you misunderstood the chapter; for, if you draw a perpendicular line from my zenith and another from the parallel of the city of Lisbon, which lies forty degrees from the equator,[15] you will clearly see that [. . .] a part of the world or the [. . .] orbit;[16] reasoning which is ill-suited to demonstrate the degrees of latitude I traversed.

Also they slander me because I said that those inhabitants prize neither gold nor other riches which we value and hold in great esteem, arguing that contrary to this we said we bought slaves from them: which strikes me as a question with so little foundation to it that in responding to it I feel I am wasting my time, paper and ink, for he who raised such a question to you would be more aptly called a *metamastician* than a mathematician;[17] for, as I said, their life is rather more Epicurean than Stoic or Academic, because, as I state, they hold no private property, nor have they divisions into kingdoms or provinces: in conclusion, all that they have they hold in common, and if they gave us, or, as I said, sold us slaves, it was not a sale for pecuniary profit, but almost given for free, because they gave us a [. . .] head[18] for a wooden comb or a twopenny mirror, and not for all the gold in the world would they have given up that comb or mirror. We tried many times to give them little gold crosses or rings with stones, but they did not want them; and also, they have this characteristic: that when we asked them for the most precious objects they have, they would give them away without asking for anything in return. And I can cite witnesses to this: that when I was making discoveries for the Sovereigns of Castile, the second voyage set us down in a land where we acquired 119 marks of pearls, which were valued in Castile at fifteen thousand ducats, and do not suppose they cost the value of ten. And when I gave a bell to an Indian, he gave me 157 pearls, later valued at a thousand ducats, and do not suppose he deemed this a poor sale, because the moment he had the bell he put it in his mouth and went off into the forest, and I never saw him again: I think he feared that I might change my mind; and many other things happened that you would marvel at were I to tell you them. So I conclude that all their wealth consists of feathers, fish bones, and other similar things: possessed not for wealth, but for ornament when they go to play games or make war. Because when I maintain that they make war, one people against the other, and that they capture one another, it may seem to a detractor that I contradict myself, since warring and capturing can come only from a desire to dominate and from the greed for temporal goods: know that they do it for none of these reasons; and when I wished to learn from them the cause of their wars, they replied that they knew nothing but that *in ancient times* their forefathers had done so, and they did so themselves for the sake of their memory; nor did they offer me any other reason, and I believe they do it in order to eat each other, as they do, their common food being human flesh: a cruel and irrational practice. On this subject let this suffice.

You ask me as well how I passed beyond the equator by compass or needle without lodestone. I answer you that the needle still pointed to the north, except that it moved one quarter to the northwest; and this we knew because the tail of the needle always pointed to the Antarctic Pole, although it took a quarter of the southeast, and we always sailed with the same needle: and in conclusion, the lodestone does not vary in the south more than in the north.

As for the description of climates, you tell me that I should have described them precisely; I marvel that you did not answer for me. For, if we, in this our hemisphere have the beginning, the middle, and the end of each climate, and the planets move through their orbits in one hemisphere as in the other, and the stars of the eighth sphere [. . .], you might have answered that the beginning, middle, and end of the first and the seventh climate are in that latitude of the equator as they are in this our hemisphere. And on this subject let this suffice. As for the semi-diurnal and seminocturnal arc and the explanation of the time I spent in those regions, it seems to me a question of little worth and less substance: for, having been in that region nine months and seven days I saw all the arcs of the brevity and length of days and of nights, and I do not know what ignorant person asks you such a thing about a familiar letter, for to tell you the truth, it does me too much honor to think that my letter should be treated as a great composition, whereas I wrote it haphazardly, as familiar letters are written. But all in all I put my trust in God's goodness, that He will grant me three years more of life to write, with the help of some scholar, something by which I might survive for a time after my death. And as for the semidiurnal and seminocturnal arcs, I noticed many times, comparing the movement of the sun, and measuring its arc with the clock, and I do not mean only a single day, but fifty, as many know [. . .].

Amerigo Vespucci

LETTER V

*Amerigo Vespucci to Lorenzo di Pierfrancesco de' Medici,
with many salutations.*

In the past I have written to you in rather ample detail about my return from those new regions which we searched for and discovered with the fleet, at the expense and orders of His Most Serene Highness the King of Portugal,[1] and which can be called a new world,[2] since our ancestors had no knowledge of them and they are entirely new matter to those who hear about them. Indeed, it surpasses the opinion of our ancient authorities, since most of them assert that there is no continent south of the equator, but merely that sea which they called the Atlantic; furthermore, if any of them did affirm that a continent was there, they gave many arguments to deny that it was habitable land. But this last voyage of mine has demonstrated that this opinion of theirs is false and contradicts all truth, since I have discovered a continent in those southern regions that is inhabited by more numerous peoples and animals than in our Europe, or Asia or Africa,[3] and in addition I found a more temperate and pleasant climate than in any other region known to us, as you will learn from what follows, where we shall briefly write only of the main points of the matter, and of those things more worthy of note and record, which I either saw or heard in this new world, as will be evident below.

We set out from Lisbon under favorable conditions on 14 May 1501[4] by order of the aforesaid king, with three ships, to go in quest of new regions to the south, and we sailed steadily for twenty months,[5] and the route was as follows. We sailed to what were formerly called the Fortunate Islands and are now the Grand Canary Islands, which are in the third climate and at the bounds of the inhabited West.[6] From there, we travelled on the Ocean Sea along the entire African coast and part of the Ethiopian, as far as the Ethiopian promontory, as Ptolemy called it,[7] which is now called Cape Verde by our people, and Bezeguiche[8] by the Ethiopians. The region is Mandanga, fourteen degrees north of the equator within the Torrid Zone, and it is inhabited by black tribes and peoples. There, once we had recovered our strength and procured all the necessities for our voyage, we weighed anchor and spread our sails to the winds; and set our course across the very vast Ocean toward the Antarctic, steering somewhat to the west with the wind known as Vulturnus:[9] and from the day we left the aforesaid promontory, we sailed for two months and three days[10] before sighting any land. What we suffered in that vast expanse of sea, what dangers of shipwreck, what physical discomforts we endured, what anxieties beset our spirits, I leave to the understanding of those who have learned well and from much experience what it means to quest after uncertain things, things they have dared to investigate without prior knowledge of them. And that I might condense the whole story into one sentence, know that out of the sixty-seven days[11] we sailed, we had forty-four continuous days of rain, thunder, and lightning, so dark that we never saw sunlight in the day, nor clear sky at night. Fear so overwhelmed us that we had almost abandoned all hope of survival. However, in those frequent, terrible tempests of sea and sky, it pleased the Most High to show us a nearby continent, and new regions and an unknown world. Sighting them, we were filled with joy, which, as one can well imagine, seizes those who have found safety after calamities and misfortunes. Thus, on 7 August 1501,[12] we dropped anchor off the shores of those regions, thanking our God with solemn prayer and the singing of a Mass. There we learned that the land was not an island but a continent, both because it extends over very long, straight shorelines, and because it is filled with countless inhabitants. For in it we encountered innumerable peoples and tribes, and all kinds of sylvan animals not found in our regions, and many other things we had never seen before, which would take too long to describe individually. God's mercy shone about greatly when we entered those regions; for our firewood and water supplies were dwindling, and in a few days we might have perished at sea. Honor be to Him, and glory, and thanks.

We decided to sail along the shore of that continent to the east, and never to lose sight of it. Soon we came to a bend where the shore curved to the south: the distance from where we first touched land to this bend was about three hundred leagues. In this phase of the voyage we landed on several occasions and conversed in friendly fashion with the people, as you will hear below. I had forgot to write to you that from the promontory of Cape Verde to the start of that continent is a distance of about seven hundred leagues, although I estimate that we sailed more than eighteen hundred, owing in part to our ignorance of the place and the ignorance of the pilot, and in part because of the storms and winds which blocked our direct course and forced us to make frequent turns. For if my companions had not relied upon me and my knowledge of cosmography, there would have been no pilot or captain on the voyage to know within five hundred leagues where we were. Indeed, we were wandering with uncertainty, with only the instruments to show us accurate altitudes of the heavenly bodies: those instruments being the quadrant and astrolabe, as everyone knows. After this, everyone held me in great honor. For I truly showed them that, without any knowledge of sea charts, I was still more expert in the science of navigation than all the pilots in the world: for they know nothing of any places beyond those where they have often sailed before. In any case, where the aforementioned bend in the land curved southward on the coast, we agreed to sail beyond it and explore what was in those regions. Therefore we sailed along the shore, approximately six hundred leagues, and we often landed and conversed with the inhabitants of those regions, and were warmly received by them, and sometimes stayed with them fifteen or twenty days at a time, always in a very friendly and hospitable way, as you will hear in the following. Part of that new continent lies in the Torrid Zone beyond the equator and toward the Antarctic Pole; it starts eight degrees beyond the equator.[13] We sailed along the shore until we passed the Tropic of Capricorn and found the Antarctic Pole, fifty degrees above their horizon, and we were 17½ degrees from the Antarctic Circle itself; I shall now relate in due order what we saw there and what we learned of those peoples' nature, customs, and tractability, and of the fertility of soil, salubriousness of climate, the dispositions of the heavens and the heavenly bodies, and in particular of the fixed stars of the eighth sphere, which our ancestors never saw or described.

First, then, the people. We found such a great multitude of people in those regions that no one could count their number (as one reads in the book of the *Apocalypse*);[14] a gentle, tractable people. Everyone of both sexes goes about naked, covering no part of the body, and just as they issued from their mothers' wombs so they go about until their dying day. They have big, solid, well-formed and well-proportioned bodies, and their complexions tend toward red, which happens, I suppose, because in going about naked they are colored by the sun.[15] They also have long[16] black hair. They are nimble in gait and in their games, and have open, pleasant faces, which they themselves, however, disfigure. They pierce their own cheeks, lips, noses, and ears, and you must not imagine that these holes are small or that they have but one of them: indeed I saw several people who had seven holes in a single face, each big enough to hold a plum. They fill these holes with beautiful stones, cerulean, marblelike, crystalline, or alabaster, or with very white bones and other things artfully wrought in their fashion;[17] if you were to see such an unusual and monstrous thing as a man with seven stones just in his cheeks or jaws or lips, some of them half a palm long, you would be amazed. And I often considered this and judged that seven such stones must weigh sixteen ounces. Beyond that, in each ear, which they pierce with three holes, they carry more stones dangling from rings; this custom is only for the men: the women do not pierce their faces, but only their ears. They have another custom that is appalling and passes belief. Their women, being very lustful, make their husbands' members swell to such thickness that they look ugly and misshapen; this they accomplish with a certain device they have and by bites from certain poisonous animals. Because of this, many men lose their members, which rot through neglect, and they are left eunuchs. They have no cloth of wool, linen, or cotton, since they need none. Nor have they private property, but own everything in common: they live together without a king and without authorities, each man his own master. They take as many wives as they wish, and son may couple with mother, brother with sister, cousin with cousin, and in general men with women as they chance to meet. They dissolve marriage as often as they please, observing no order in any of these matters. Moreover, they have no temple and no religion, nor do they worship idols. What more can I say? They live according to nature, and might be called Epicureans rather than Stoics.[18] There are no merchants among them, nor is there any commerce. The peoples make war among themselves without art or order. The elders deliver orations to the young to sway their will, urging them on to wars in which they kill each other cruelly, and they take captives and keep them, not to spare them, but to kill them for food: for they eat each other, the victors eat the vanquished, and together with other kinds of meat, human flesh is common fare among them. This you may be sure of, because one father was known to have eaten his children and wife,[19] and I myself met and spoke with a man who was said to have eaten more than three hundred[20] human bodies; and I also stayed twenty-seven days in a certain city in which I saw salted human flesh hanging from house-beams, much as we hang up bacon and pork. I will say more: they marvel that we do not eat our enemies and use their flesh as food, for they say human flesh is very savory. Their weapons are bows and arrows, and when they charge into battle, they cover no part of their bodies to protect themselves, also in this respect like animals. We tried our best to dissuade them from these wicked customs, and they promised us that they would give them up. Their women, as I said, although they go naked and are exceedingly lustful, still have rather shapely and clean bodies, and are not as revolting as one might think, because, being fleshy, their shameful parts are less visible, covered for the most part by the good quality of their bodily composition. It seemed remarkable to us that none of them appeared to have sagging breasts, and also, those who had borne children could not be distinguished from the virgins by the shape or tautness of their wombs, and this was true too of other parts of their bodies, which decency bids me pass over.[21] When they were able to copulate with Christians, they were driven by their excessive lust to corrupt and prostitute all their modesty. The people live to be 150 years old,[22] seldom fall ill, and if they do happen to contract some sickness, they cure themselves with certain roots of herbs. These are the more remarkable things I noticed among them. The air there is very temperate and good, and, as I was able to learn by conversing with the people, there is no pestilence or illness there deriving from contaminated air, and unless they die a violent death, they live a long life: I think this is due to the southern winds blowing constantly there, especially the one we call Eurus,[23] which is to them as Aquilo[24] is to us. They are very zealous fishermen, and the sea there is full of fish of all sorts.[25] They are not hunters: I think this is because there are many kinds of forest animals there, especially lions,[26] bears, countless snakes, and other dreadful and ill-formed beasts, and forests on all sides with trees of enormous size, that they do not dare to expose themselves, naked and without any protection or weapons, to such dangers.

The land of those regions is very fertile and pleasant, abundant in hills and mountains, countless valleys and huge rivers, watered by healthful springs, and filled with broad, dense, barely penetrable forests and all sorts of wild beasts. Great trees grow there without cultivation, and many of them produce fruits delicious to taste and beneficial to the human body, though several indeed are the opposite, and none of the fruits there are like our own. Numberless kinds of herbs and roots grow there as well, from which the people make bread and excellent foods. They also have many seeds, totally different from ours. There are no kinds of metal there except gold, in which those regions abound, although we did not bring any back with us on this our first voyage. The inhabitants apprised us of it, and told us that in the interior there is great abundance of gold, which they do not at all value or consider precious. They are rich in pearls, as I wrote to you elsewhere.[27] If I wanted to mention separately all the things which are there, and to write about the numerous kinds of animals and their great numbers, I would grow too prolix with a matter so vast; and I certainly believe that our Pliny did not come within a thousandth part of the types of parrots and other birds and animals which are in those regions, with such great diversity of forms and colors that even Polycletus,[28] master of painting in all its perfection, would have failed to depict them adequately. All the trees there are fragrant, and all produce gum or oil or some liquor, and I do not doubt that their properties, if they were known to us, would be salubrious for the human body; and certainly, if anywhere in the world there exists an Earthly Paradise, I think it is not far from those regions, which lie, as I said, to the south, and in such a temperate climate that they never have either icy winters or scorching summers.

Sky and air are clear for most of the year and free from dense vapors. The rains there fall delicately and last three or four hours, then vanish like mist. The sky is adorned with very beautiful signs and figures, in which I noticed twenty stars as bright as we sometimes see Venus or Jupiter. I considered their movements and orbits and measured their circumferences and diameters with geometric methods, and determined that they are of great magnitude. I saw three Canopi[29] in that sky, two of which are bright indeed, and the third dim. The Antarctic Pole has no Ursa Major and Ursa Minor, as appear in our Arctic Pole, nor is any bright star seen near it; of the stars which are carried around it in smaller orbit, there are three which form the figure of an orthogonal triangle, of which half the circumference, or the diameter, is 9½ degrees. As they rise, a white

Canopus of extraordinary size can be seen to the left. When they
reach mid-heaven they form this figure:

```
      *                          s s
                               s s s s
                             s s s s s s
                               s s s s
                                              Canopus
      *                          *
```

After these come two other stars, of which half the circumference, or diameter, is 12½ degrees, and with them can be seen
another white Canopus. Another six stars, the brightest and most
beautiful of all in the eighth sphere, follow them; on the surface of
the firmament, these stars have a half-circumference, or diameter,
of thirty-two degrees. A black Canopus of immense size soars up
with them. They are seen in the Milky Way and form a figure like
this when they are on the meridian line:

```
                        *
   *     *     *                          *
               s s
             s s s s s
            s s s s s s
              s s s
                *
```

I encountered many other very beautiful stars during this
voyage of mine, and I notated their movements carefully and have
described them beautifully and graphically in a booklet of mine.[30]
His Most Serene Highness the King has it at present, and I hope

that he will return it to me. In that hemisphere I saw things which do not agree with the arguments of philosophers: a white rainbow was seen twice around midnight, not only by me, but also by all the sailors. Likewise, several times we saw a new moon on the day when it was in conjunction with the sun. Every night in that part of the sky, innumerable vapors and bright flares streak across. A bit earlier I spoke of the hemisphere, although, properly speaking, it is not fully a hemisphere with respect to ours; but since it approaches the shape of one, it is permissible to call it so.

Therefore, as I said, from Lisbon, our point of departure, 39½ degrees from the equator, we sailed fifty degrees beyond the equator, which together make about ninety degrees, and since this sum makes a quarter of the great circle, according to the true reasoning of measurement passed on to us by the ancients, it is clear that we sailed around a quarter of the world. And by this logic, we who live in Lisbon, 39½ degrees this side of the equator in the northern latitude,[31] are at an angle of five degrees in the transverse line to those who live at the fiftieth degree beyond the same line in the southern latitude, or, so that you may understand more clearly: a perpendicular line, which hangs over our heads from a point directly above us while we stand upright, hangs pointing toward their sides or ribs: thus we are in an upright line, and they in a transverse line, and a kind of orthogonal triangle is formed thereby, of which we form the perpendicular line, they the base, and the hypothenuse extends from our vertex to theirs, as is evident in the drawing (p. 55). And let these words suffice for cosmography.

These were the more noteworthy things I saw on this last navigation of mine, which I call the "third journey." The other two "journeys" were my two other navigations, which I made toward the west on a mandate from the Most Serene King of the

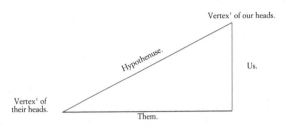

Spains;[32] on those voyages I noted the marvels accomplished by the sublime creator of all, our God: I kept a diary of the noteworthy things, so that, if ever I am granted the leisure, I may gather together all these marvels one by one and write a book, either of geography or of cosmography, so that my memory will live on for posterity, and so that the immense creation of almighty God, unknown in part to the ancients yet known to us, may be recognized. I pray, therefore, to the most merciful God that He may prolong the days of my life, that by His good grace, and for the salvation of my soul, I may attain the fullest realization of my goals. The other two "journeys" I keep among my private papers, and when the Most Serene Highness returns the "third journey" to me, I shall try to return to tranquillity and my homeland, where I will be able to confer with experts and, with the help and encouragement of my friends, to complete that work.

I ask your forgiveness for not sending you this last navigation, or rather this last "journey," as I had promised to do in my last letter: you know the reason, since I could not yet have the original back from His Most Serene Highness. I still plan to make a fourth voyage, and have already received the promise of two ships together with their equipment, so that I may prepare to search for new regions to the south, travelling from the east with the wind called Africus;[33] on this voyage I think I will accomplish many things to the praise of God, the benefit of this kingdom, and the honor of my old age; and I await nothing but the consent of His Most Serene Highness. May God permit whatever is for the best. You will learn of whatever happens.

The interpreter Giocondo[34] has translated this letter from Italian to Latin, so that all the Latins may understand how many marvelous things are being discovered every day, and to curb the audacity of those people who wish to study the heavens and their majesty and to know more than they are permitted to know, for, ever since the world began, the earth's vastness and all things contained in it have been unknown.

Praise to God.

LETTER VI

Letter of Amerigo Vespucci concerning the islands newly discovered on his four voyages.

Magnificent Lord, After humble reverence and due salutations, etc. Well may Your Magnificence marvel at my temerity
and brazen boldness with which I am so absurdly bestirred to
write to Your Magnificence the present quite prolix letter, while
knowing that Your Magnificence is forever occupied with high
counsels and vexing affairs pertaining to the good government of
that sublime Republic; you will deem me not merely presumptuous, but also frivolous in setting about to write things little
befitting your station, nor are they delightful, but written in a
barbarous style well beneath any standard of humane discourse.
Yet the faith I have in your virtues and in the truth of my writing, for these are things not to be found in the ancient or
modern writers, as Your Magnificence will find in the following,
emboldens me.

The principal cause that moved me to write to you was the
request of the present letter-bearer, one Benvenuto Benvenuti, a
fellow Florentine, very much at Your Magnificence's service, as
he shows himself to be, and very much my friend. He, on finding
himself here in this city of Lisbon, entreated me to impart to Your
Magnificence those things which I have seen in various regions of
the world by virtue of four voyages which I made to discover new
lands: and two were by command of the exalted King of Castile,

Don Fernando VI,[1] to go west over the depths of the Ocean Sea, and the other two were by command of the mighty King Don Manuel of Portugal,[2] to go south; Benvenuti telling me that Your Magnificence would take pleasure in it, and that in this he hoped to serve you. For which reason I have set about the task, for I am sure that Your Magnificence counts me among the number of his servants, since I remember how, in the time of our youth, I was your friend, just as I am now your servant, and how we would go to hear the principles of grammar[3] exampled in the good life and doctrine of the venerable religious friar of San Marco, fra' Giorgio Antonio Vespucci, my uncle;[4] and would to God I had followed his counsels and doctrine, for, as Petrarch says, I would be "another man from that which I am."[5] Be that as it may, I have no regrets, because I have always delighted in virtuous things; and if this empty chatter of mine be unworthy of your virtues, I shall say to you as Pliny said to Maecenas:[6] "Once you were wont to take pleasure in my prattle." And continually occupied as Your Magnificence must be with public concerns, still you must reserve some hours for recreation, and spend a little time in trifling or delightful things; and just as fennel is customarily placed on top of delicious foods to improve them for the digestion, so you will be able, to escape from your many occupations, to have this letter of mine read, so that you may take refuge somewhat from the continual care and assiduous consideration of public matters; and if I am prolix, I beg your pardon.

My Magnificent Lord, Your Magnificence must know that the motive for my coming here to the kingdom of Spain was to engage in trade,[7] and as I pursued this goal for about four years, during which I witnessed and experienced the varied workings of fortune, marking how she shifts about these ephemeral and transient things, and how she one time holds a man at the top of her wheel, and another time tosses him away from her and strips him of all those goods which can be said to have been borrowed; so that, having known the continual struggle man undergoes to acquire possessions, subjecting himself to so many hardships and dangers, I decided to abandon trading and set my sights upon something more praiseworthy and enduring: so it was that I determined to go to see part of the world and its wonders. And to this end a very propitious time and occasion offered themselves to me: for it so happened that, when King Don Fernando of Castile was planning to dispatch four ships to discover new lands to the west, I was chosen by His Highness to accompany that fleet to assist in the discoveries. And we departed from the port of Cadiz on 10 May 1497, and wended our way upon the great depths of the Ocean Sea; we were seventeen months[8] upon this voyage and discovered much continental land and countless isles, and a great part of them inhabited, which are not spoken about by the ancient writers, I believe because they had no knowledge of them: for, if I remember correctly, in some one of them which I read it was held that this Ocean Sea was unpeopled,[9] and our own poet Dante was of this opinion, when in the twenty-sixth chapter of the *Inferno*, he depicts the death of Ulysses. On this voyage I saw things of great wonder, as Your Magnificence shall hear.

As I said above, we departed from the port of Cadiz in four convoy ships, and we began our navigation bound for the Fortunate Islands, which are now called the Canary Islands, and are situated in the Ocean Sea at the end of the inhabited west,[10] located in the third climate, above which the North Pole rises 27½ degrees, and they are 280 leagues from this city of Lisbon on a course between south and southwest; where we remained eight days, provisioning ourselves with water and firewood and other necessities. From this point, having said our prayers, we weighed anchor and set our sails to the wind, starting our navigation on a course west by south. We sailed until, at the end of thirty-seven days, we came to a land that we judged to be mainland; which lies to the west of the Canary Islands, about a thousand leagues beyond the inhabited west and within the Torrid Zone, for we found the North Pole to rise over its horizon sixteen degrees, and it was seventy-five degrees farther west than the Canary Islands,[11] according to what our instruments showed.

In that place we anchored with our ships, a league and a half from land, and cast down our boats, crowded with men and arms, and turned in the direction of the land. And before we had reached it, we sighted many people ambling along the beach, which cheered us greatly, and we found these people to be naked. They showed that they were afraid of us, I believe because they saw that we were clothed and of different stature. They all withdrew into the woods, and, despite all the signs we made to them of peace and friendship, they did not wish to come to parley with us; so that, as night was coming on, and the ships were anchored in a dangerous spot and stood along the open coast unprotected, we resolved to remove ourselves from there the next day and go in search of some port or cove where we might secure our ships.

We sailed on to the northwest, for the coast ran that way, we stayed always in sight of land, and all the while we could see people upon the beach, until, having sailed for two days, we found quite safe mooring for the ships, and anchored half a league from land, where we saw a great many people. And the same day we ventured ashore in the boats, and landed a full crew of forty in good order; and the people on land still showed their disdain to converse with us, and we could not reassure them enough to come and speak with us. And that day we took such pains to give them some of our things, such as bells, mirrors, glass beads, and other trifles, that at length some of them were reassured and came to trade with us. And having entered on friendly terms with them, as night came on we took leave of them and returned to the ships. And the next day, at the crack of dawn, we saw countless people standing on the beach, and they had brought with them their women and children. We went ashore and found that all these women were laden with their provisions, which will be described in due course in this letter. And before we had reached land, many of them threw themselves into the sea and came swimming the distance of a crossbow shot to greet us, for they are quite excellent swimmers, and this trust of theirs was most gratifying.

What we came to know of their life and ways[12] was that they go about completely naked, the men and as well as the women, without covering any shame, exactly as they emerged from their mothers' wombs. They are of medium stature, very well proportioned; their skin is a color that tends toward red like lion's fur, and I believe that if they went about clothed, they would be white like us.[13] They have no hair on their body but for long black hair on their heads, the women especially, which makes them beautiful. They are not very fair of countenance, for they have broad faces somewhat reminiscent of the Tartars, they do not allow any hair to grow on their brows or eyelids, nor in any other part, except the head, because they consider bodily hair an ugly thing. They are very nimble in their walking and running, the men as well as the women, so that a women thinks nothing of running a league or two, for many times we saw them do just that, and in this they have a very great advantage over us Christians. They swim unbelievably, and the women are better than the men, for many times we encountered and saw them swimming about two leagues out to sea without any support.

Their weapons are very well made bows and arrows, but for the fact that they do not have iron or any other sort of hard metal, and in place of iron they use the teeth of animals or fish, or a scorched twig of hard wood;[14] they are sure bowsmen, striking where they aim, and in some parts the women also use these bows. They have other weapons, such as fire-hardened spears and other extremely well crafted clubs with heads. They make war with people who speak another language, and do so very cruelly, without sparing anyone's life, unless they keep them alive to inflict still greater suffering upon them. When they go to war, they take their women with them, not to make them fight but to carry the provisions, for a women carries a load upon her that a man could not bear, thirty or forty leagues, as we saw many times. They are not accustomed to having any captain, nor do they march in battle order, for each man is his own master. And the cause of their wars is not the desire to rule, or to extend their boundaries, or any inordinate greed, but merely an ancient enmity which has existed among them since olden times; and when we asked them why they warred, they could give no other reason than that they did it to avenge the death of their ancestors and their fathers. These people have neither king nor lord, nor do they obey anyone, for they live in their own liberty; and they are moved to go to war when the enemies have killed or captured one of them, and his eldest relative rises up and goes preaching through the streets that they should follow after him to avenge the death of that relative of his: and in this way they are moved to compassion.

They do not practice justice nor do they punish the wrongdoer, nor do father and mother punish their children, and rarely or never did we observe a quarrel take place among them. They appear to speak simply, and are very cunning and clever in the matters that concern them. They speak tersely, in a low voice; they have the same accentuation as we do, for they form their words either with the palate or with the teeth or the tongue, but they use other names for things. There are many different languages, for every hundred leagues we found the language change, each one mutually incomprehensible to the other.

Their way of life is very barbarous, for they do not eat at specific hours, but when and however often they want, and it matters little to them if their appetite comes at midnight rather than during the day, since they eat at all hours. And they eat on the ground without tablecloth or any other sort of napkin, for they have no such things; they keep their food in earthen bowls of their own manufacture, or in halves of gourds. They sleep in certain nets made of heavy cotton, very big and suspended in the air; and although this way of sleeping of theirs may seem bad, I can tell you that it is a good way to sleep, for countless times we happened to sleep in these nets, and we all slept better than on mattresses. They are clean and neat in their persons, for they are continually washing themselves. When they evacuate (with all respect) their bowels, they do their utmost not to be seen; and as neat and fastidious as they are in this, in making water they are filthy and shameless, the men as well as the women, for while standing and talking with us, without turning away or showing shame they would release that foulness, since in this they have no shame whatsoever.

There are no marriages among them; each man takes as many women as he wants, and when he wishes to repudiate them, he does so, without it being deemed an injustice to him or a disgrace to the woman, for in this matter the woman has as much liberty as the man. They are not very jealous, and are inordinately lustful, the women much more than the men, though decency bids us pass over the wiles they employ to satisfy their inordinate lust. These women are very fertile women and their pregnancies do not exempt them from any work whatsoever; and their deliveries are so easy that a day after giving birth, they go out as usual, and especially to wash themselves in the river,[15] and are fit as fish. They are so unmoved by love and so cruel that, if they grow angry with their husbands, they immediately make a potion with which to kill the child in their wombs and abort;[16] and on this account they kill innumerable children. They are women of noble body, very well proportioned, for one does not find on their bodies any ill-formed member or thing; and although they go about completely naked, they are fleshy women, and one does not see that part of their shame which he who has not seen these women can imagine, for they cover everything with their thighs, except for that part for which nature did not provide, which is, to speak discreetly, the pubis: in conclusion, they are no more shamed by their shameful parts than we are in showing our nose or mouth. Seldom will you see sagging breasts on a woman, or a womb sagging from repeated childbirths, or other wrinkles,[17] for they all seem as though they never gave birth. They showed themselves to be very desirous to copulate with us Christians.

We do not encounter among these peoples any who had a religion, nor can they be called Moors or Jews, and are worse than heathens, because we never saw them perform any sacrifice, nor did they have any house of prayer:[18] I judge their life to be Epicurean.

Their dwellings are communal, and their houses are built like huts, but sturdily made and constructed out of very big trees and covered with palm leaves, safe from storms and winds, and in some places so wide and long that we found six hundred souls in a single house; and a village we saw had only thirteen houses in which dwelt four thousand souls. Every eight or ten years they change their villages,[19] and asked why they put themselves to so much effort, they gave a natural answer: they said that they did this because of the soil, which, from too much filth, became infected and corrupted and caused illness in their bodies; which seemed to us a good reason.

Their wealth consists of birds' feathers of many colors, and strands of beads they make out of fish bones or white and green stones, which they hang from their cheeks and from their lips and ears, and many other things which we do not value at all. They do not engage in commerce, neither buying nor selling: in short, they live and content themselves with whatever nature gives them. The wealth to which we are accustomed in this Europe of ours and in other parts, such as gold, jewels, pearls, and other riches, are of no interest to them, although they have them in their lands, they neither labor to procure them, nor prize them. They are liberal in giving, and rarely deny you anything, and conversely are liberal in asking, once they have demonstrated that they are your friends; for the great token of friendship they will show you is to give you their women and their young daughters, and a father or mother who has brought you a daughter, even when she is a young virgin, deems it a great honor that you sleep with her; and in this they make the highest show of friendship.

When they die, they observe various forms of obsequies, and some are buried with water or food laid by their heads,[20] since they think they will need to eat: they do not have or perform ceremonies with candles or lamentations. In some other areas they have the most barbarous and inhuman form of burial: which is that when one who is suffering or sick is almost at death's door, his relatives take him into a big forest, and set up between two trees one of those nets of theirs for sleeping, and they place him in it and dance around him for a whole day; and when night comes, they set water and various foods by his bedside, enough for him to maintain himself for four to six days, and then they leave him all alone and return to the village. And if the sick man helps himself and eats and drinks and survives, he returns to the village, and his relatives receive him with ceremony; but few survive in this fashion: without being further visited they die, and that is their burial. And they have many other customs which to avoid prolixity will not be mentioned.

In their sickness they use various types of medicine, so different from ours that we marvelled that anyone survived; for, many times I saw that they bathe a man sick with a rising fever from head to toe, after which they made a big fire around him, and turned him over again and again for two hours more, until, having tired him out they let him sleep; and thus many were cured. Along with this, they frequently practice fasting, for they go three days without eating, and also bloodletting, but not from the arm, rather from the thighs, the haunches, and the calves. Likewise they induce vomiting with herbs which they put in their mouth. And they use many other remedies it would take much time to relate.

They are far too phlegmatic and sanguine because of their food, which largely consists of roots, herbs, fruit, and fish. They do not have seeds for wheat or other grains, and for their usual eating fare they use the root a tree from which they make flour, rather good, which they call yucca,[21] and other roots called cassava,[22] and still others yams.[23] They eat little meat, except for human flesh: for Your Magnificence must know that in this they are so inhuman that they surpass all bestial ways, since they eat all the enemies that they kill or capture, female as well as male, with such ferocity that merely to speak of it seems a brute thing—how much more to see it, as befell me countless times, in many places. And they marvelled to hear us say that we do not eat our enemies, and this Your Magnificence should believe for certain: their other barbarous customs are so many that speech fails to describe such facts.

And because during these four voyages I saw so many things unlike our customs, I set about writing a commonplace book which I call *The Four Journeys*, in which I have related quite precisely most of the things which I saw, as far as my weak wit brought me; which book I have not yet published, because I find my own things so little to my liking that I find no savor in what I wrote, although many encourage me to publish it. Everything will be found minutely accounted in the book, so I shall not elaborate further in this chapter, since we shall come in the course of this letter to many other particulars; let this suffice then by its generalities.

In this initial stage we did not see anything very profitable in the land, except some signs of gold: I believe this was because we did not know the language, for the position and the condition of the land could not be better.

We decided to leave from there and go further on, coasting continually along the land, in which we made many stops and conversed with many people; and after several days we found ourselves before a harbor where we faced very great danger, yet it pleased the Holy Spirit to save us, and this is what occurred. We were entering a port, where we found a village built upon the water like Venice:[24] there were about forty-four large houses shaped like huts, supported by huge poles, and they had their doors, or rather the house entrances, rigged like drawbridges; and from one house one could go to all the others, by dint of the drawbridges which extended from house to house. And when the people of those houses saw us, they showed themselves to be afraid of us, and forthwith drew up all the bridges. And while we witnessed this wonder, we saw coming upon the sea about twenty-two canoes, which is the kind of vessel they use, made from single trees, and these were advancing in the direction of our boats, and as they marvelled at our features and clothing, they kept their distance. So we signalled to them to come to us, reassuring them with every sign of friendship; and since they did not come to us, we approached them, and they did not wait for us, but returned to the shore, motioning to us that we should wait and they would return immediately; and they went behind a hill and did not take long. When they returned they were leading sixteen of their girls, and got into their canoes with the girls and came up to our boats, and in each boat they placed four girls, an act which greatly astonished us, as Your Magnificence can well imagine; they arranged their canoes among our boats, coming up to us and speaking with us, which we judged to be a sign of friendship. And while we were thus occupied we saw many people swimming through the sea, who were coming out of the houses; and as they approached us, without our suspecting anything, certain old women appeared at the doors of the houses raising very loud cries, pulling their hair, and exhibiting great sorrow. That raised our suspicion, and each of us reached for our weapons; and all at once the girls we had in our boats leapt into the sea, and the men in the canoes moved away from us and started to shoot at us with their bows; and all those who had come swimming up to us held lances below the water, concealing them as best they could. Thus, having recognized their treachery, we began not only to defend ourselves against them, but fiercely to assail them, and we sank many of their *almadías*,[25] or canoes, as they call them, with our boats; we made massacre of them, and all plunged into the water to swim away: leaving their canoes abandoned, with heavy losses for them as they were swimming toward land. About fifteen or twenty were killed, and many were wounded; and of our men five were wounded and all survived, by the grace of God. We captured two of the girls and three men, and headed for their houses, and once inside, found only two old women and one sick man. We took many things from them, though of little value, and we preferred not to burn down their houses, since it seemed to us something that would burden our consciences; and we returned to our boats with five prisoners, and headed back to the ships, and put a pair of irons on the feet of each of the prisoners, except for the young girls; and that night the two girls and one of the men managed to escape by the most artful way in the world.

And the next day we resolved to leave that harbor and go farther on. Sailing continually along the coast, we caught sight of another people living perhaps eighty leagues from these others, and we found them quite different in language and customs. We decided to anchor and went ashore in our boats and saw many people standing on the beach, perhaps close to four thousand souls. And when we reached land, they did not await us and took flight into the woods, abandoning their things. We jumped ashore and followed a path into the forest, and at the distance of a crossbow shot found their huts, where they had built huge fires over which they were cooking their food and roasting many animals and various kinds of fish; we saw that they were roasting a certain animal which seemed to be a dragon, except that it had no wings,[26] and was so hideous in aspect that we marvelled greatly at its fearsomeness. In this fashion we went through their houses, or rather huts, and found many of these serpents alive, bound by their feet and with a cord wound around their snouts so that they could not open their mouths, as we do with mastiffs so that they do not bite. They were so fierce in appearance that none of us dared to take one, thinking they were poisonous. They are as big as a kid and a braccio and a half long; they have big long feet, armed with large claws; they have tough skin and are of different colors; the snout and face are like a serpent's, and starting at the nose a crest runs down them like a saw, along the middle of their backs to the tip of their tail: in short, we judged that they were poisonous serpents, yet these people ate them. We found that they made bread out of little fish[27] which they caught in the sea, first boiling the creatures, then piling them up to knead a dough or bread with them, and they would roast them over coals: thus they ate them. We tried it and found that it was good. They had so many other sorts of food, especially so many sorts of fruits and roots, that it would be a lengthy matter to recount them all in detail. When we noticed that the people did not come back, we decided not to touch or take anything of theirs, the better to reassure them; and we left many of our things in their huts where they could see them, and returned for the night to the ships.

At next daybreak, we saw countless people on the beach, and we went ashore; and although they still showed that they were fearful of us, yet they were sufficiently reassured to trade with us, giving us all that we asked of them and showing themselves to be our very good friends. They told us that these were not their dwellings, and that they had come there to do their fishing, and they asked us to come to their dwellings and villages, because they wanted to receive us as friends; and they acted in such friendly fashion because the two men whom we were holding captive were their enemies. So that, noting their great insistence, conferring among ourselves, twenty-eight of us Christians agreed to go with them in good order and with firm purpose, and if necessary, to die manfully. And after spending almost three days there, we departed with them for the interior; and three leagues from the beach we came to a village with a good many people and few houses (there were not more than nine), where we were received with so many, and such barbarous, ceremonies that the pen can but fail to describe them: these included dances and songs and laments mixed with mirth and many foods. And there we spent the night, where they offered us their women, and we were unable to fend them off.

And having passed the night and half the next day there, so many tribes came to see us and marvel at us, that they were beyond counting; and the elders requested that we go with them to other villages, farther into the interior, indicating that they would do us the greatest honor. For which reason we agreed to go, and it is impossible to tell how much honor they did heap upon us; and we visited so many villages that we were nine days underway, so long that our fellow Christians who had stayed behind at the ships were already concerned about us. And finding ourselves about eighteen leagues inland, we decided that we should return to the ships; and at our return so many people, men and women alike, came with us all the way to the sea, that it was a wondrous thing; and if any of our men grew tired along the way, they would lift him most comfortably, and at crossing of rivers, which abound there and are very big, by their devices they got us across so safely that we were well out of any danger.[28] Many of them came laden with the things which they had given us, among which, their sleeping nets and very rich plumage, many bows and arrows, innumerable parrots of various colors; and others brought with them stores of provisions and animals; and I shall tell you a greater marvel still: that the one who, at the water crossings, had to carry us over on his back considered himself lucky thereby.

And having reached the sea, our boats arrived and we boarded them, and they in their eagerness to enter the boats and see our ships formed so great a crowd that they flooded them. And we took as many as we could in the boats, and went to the ships, and so many came swimming that we felt uneasy to see so many people on the ships, for there were more than a thousand souls, all naked and unarmed: they were marvelling at our instruments and our equipment and the size of the ships. And something very humorous occurred with them on board, namely that we decided to discharge some of our artillery; and when the report rang out, most of them jumped overboard in fear: just as frogs on a bank upon noticing something frightening will jump into the pond, so did these people;[29] and those who remained on the ships remained so frightened that we regretted such a deed: yet we reassured them by telling them that we killed our enemies with those weapons. And having idled away the entire day on the ships, we told them they would have to go away, because we wanted to leave that night; and thus, they parted from us in great friendship and love, and returned to shore.

Among these people and on their land I met and saw so many of their customs and ways of living that I do not wish to elaborate on them: for Your Magnificence must know that I have made note of the most wondrous things on each of my voyages, and have gathered them all together in one volume in the style of a geography, which I have entitled *The Four Journeys,* a little work that contains everything in detail, though a copy has not yet been published, because I need to confer with experts.

This land is very heavily populated both with many people and countless rivers; few of the animals resemble ours, except for lions, jaguars, deer, hogs, roe deer and does, and even these are somewhat different. They have neither horses, nor mules, nor (with all respect) asses, nor dogs, nor sheep nor any sort of cattle; yet the animals they do have are so numerous, and all are wild, and they use none of them for work, that it would be impossible to enumerate them. What are we to say of the birds, of there which there are so many and so many sorts and colors of plumage that is a marvel to behold them? The land is very pleasant and fertile, filled with huge woods and forests, and always green, for the leaves never fall. The fruits are so many that they are beyond counting and unlike any of ours. This land lies within the Torrid Zone, near to or below the parallel which bounds the Tropic of Cancer, where the pole rises twenty-three degrees over the horizon and the end of the second climate.

Many tribes came to see us, and marvelled at our features and our whiteness; and they asked us whence we came, and we gave them to understand that we came from heaven,[30] and that we were going to see the world, and they believed it. In this land we set up a baptismal fount, and baptized countless people; and in their language they called us *carabi*,[31] which means 'men of great wisdom.'

We left this harbor (and the province is called Paria) and sailed along the coast always within sight of land, until we had travelled 870 leagues always to the northwest, making many stops along the way and trading with many people; and at many points we acquired gold, though not a large quantity, for it was enough that we discovered the land and learned that they had gold in it.

And when we had already spent thirteen months on the voyage, and the vessels and the equipment were quite worn out and the men tired, we held common counsel and agreed to run the ships onto shore and there careen them, since they were leaking so badly, in order to caulk and tar them again, and then return in the direction of Spain. And at the moment we decided this, we were close to reaching the best harbor in the world, which we entered with our ships, and where we found countless people, who received us with much friendship; and on land we built a bastion with the boats and tuns and casks and our artillery firing in all directions. And after unloading and lightening our ships, we hauled them ashore and repaired them in every way necessary; and the people on land helped us considerably and continuously provided us with food of theirs, for in this harbor we tasted little of our own, and this was a good turn to do us, since the provisions we had for our return were meagre and poor; we stayed there thirty-seven days and went many times to their villages, where they treated us extremely honorably. And when we were eager to set out again upon our voyage, they reminded us that at certain times of the year a very cruel people who were their enemy came by sea to their land and by treachery and force killed many of them and ate them, and some of them were captured and taken to their houses or their land, and that they could barely defend themselves from them, making signs to us that these were island people who could venture a hundred leagues out to sea. And they told us this with so much emotion that we believed them and promised to avenge them of so great a wrong; and they were very happy at this. And many of them offered to come with us, but we did not wish to take them for many reasons, except for seven whom we did take along on the condition that they follow us in their canoes, since we did not want to be obliged to return them to their land; and they were content with this.

And thus we parted from these people having made great friends of them. And with our ships repaired, we sailed out to sea seven days on a course northeast by east, and after seven days we encountered islands, which were numerous, and some inhabited and others deserted. And we anchored by one of these, where we saw many people, and they called this island Iti;[32] and with our boats full of fine men, and three mortars on each boat, we headed toward land, where we found some four hundred men and many women waiting, all of them naked like those before. They were well built and seemed quite warlike men, for they were armed with their weapons, which are bows, arrows, and spears; and most of them were holding small square shields, in such a way that they were not hindered from shooting their bows. And as we were about the distance of a bowshot from the land, they all leapt into the water, shooting arrows to prevent our landing. And all their bodies were painted with different colors, and plumed with feathers; and when they showed themselves painted and plumed as they were, this meant that they wanted to fight. And they were so obstinate in preventing us from landing that we were forced to make use of our artillery; and as they heard the report and saw saw some of their number fall dead, they all retreated inland. Whereby, after holding counsel, we decided that forty-two of us should land, and, if they were waiting for us, to fight with them. Thus when we had landed with our weapons, they came at us, and we fought for about an hour, but with little advantage over them, except that our crossbowmen and musketeers killed some of them; and they wounded some of our men; and this was because they were not waiting for us to come within range of lance or sword. And we set upon them with such force that finally they came within sword range; and when they had had a taste of our weapons, they fled into the woods and forests, and left us victorious on the field with many of their dead and still more wounded.

And that day we did not trouble to go any further after them, for we were very tired, and returned to the ships with so much joy on the part of the seven men who had come with us, that they could not contain themselves.

And the next day we saw a great number of people coming over the land, still in their battle gear, sounding horns and various other instruments which they use in their wars, and all painted and plumed, which was a very strange sight. For this reason all the ships held counsel, and it was decided, since this tribe wanted to be our enemies, that we should meet with them and do all that we could to make friends of them; in the event they should not want our friendship, we would then treat them as enemies; and as many of them as we could capture should all be our slaves. And arming ourselves as best we could, we headed toward land, and they did not prevent our landing, I believe out of fear of the mortars. And fifty-seven of our men landed in four squadrons, each captain with his own men, and we entered combat with them. And after a long battle, when many of them were dead, we put them to flight and chased them to a village, having captured around 250 of them; and we burned down the village and returned to the ships with victory and 250 prisoners, leaving many of them dead and wounded; and no more than one of our men died, and the twenty-two wounded all survived, thanks be to God.

We arranged our departure, and the seven men, five of whom were wounded, took a canoe from the island, and with seven prisoners whom we gave them—four women and three men— they returned to their land very happy, and marvelling at our powers. And we thus set sail for Spain with 222 captured slaves, and we reached the port of Cadiz on 15 October 1498, where we were well received and sold our slaves.

These are the most notable things that happened to me on my first voyage.

End of the first voyage.

The second begins.

What follows pertains to the second voyage and what I saw on it that was most worthy of memory.

We left the port of Cadiz in a convoy of three ships on 16 May 1499, and set our course for the Cape Verde Islands, passing within sight of Grand Canary Island; and we sailed until we came upon an island known as the Isle of Fire.[33] After obtaining our supplies of water and firewood, we took our course to the south-west, and in forty-four days we came upon a new land, which we judged to be mainland and connected with the land mentioned above; which is situated within the Torrid Zone and beyond the equator to the south, above which the South Pole rises five degrees beyond all climates, and is five hundred leagues in a southwesterly direction from those islands; and we found the days to be equal to the nights, because we arrived there on 27 June, when the sun is close to the Tropic of Cancer. This land we found to be completely flooded and filled with very large rivers; and the land within proved to be very green with large trees.

At the outset we did not see any people. We anchored our ships and lowered our boats; and reached shore and, as I have said, found it full of very large trees and flooded by the very large rivers we found there; and we attempted to enter the land at many points; but because of the great waters which flowed into the rivers, for all our exertions, we could not find any place not flooded by the water. Along the rivers we saw many signs that indicated that the land was populated; and since we could not enter at this point, we decided to return to the ships and try at some farther point. And returning to the ships, and weighing anchor, we sailed a course east by southeast, coasting the land continually, for it trended in that direction; and every forty leagues we attempted to enter, but each time it was in vain. We found that the sea currents were so strong along this coast that they did not permit us to navigate, and they all ran from the southeast to the northwest. So that, seeing how difficult it was to navigate, we held counsel and decided to return to our northwest course.

And we sailed along the land until we came upon a very beautiful harbor created by a large island[34] which stood at its entrance, and within it a very large bay had been formed. While sailing to its entrance, continuing along the island, we had seen many people, and cheered by this, steered our ships to be anchored where we saw the people, which might have been about four leagues out to sea. And sailing in this fashion, we had caught sight of a canoe coming over the high sea, with many people in it; and we decided to overtake it, and turned our ships toward it, with the order not to lose it.[35] And sailing toward it before a fresh wind, we observed that they were standing firm with oars lifted, I believe out of astonishment at our ships; and when they saw that we were approaching them, they lowered the oars into the water and started to head toward land. And as our company had a forty-five ton caravel which was a very good sailer, she placed herself windward of the canoe, and when it seemed the right moment to overtake it, she let out the tackle and rigging and headed in its direction, and we with it; and as the small caravel came alongside it and did want to collide with it, she passed it and then stayed downwind. And when they saw their chance, they began rowing vigorously, to flee; and we had the boats at the stern already filled with good men, thinking that they would seize that canoe. And they struggled for more than two hours, and finally, if the small caravel had not returned to windward once again, we would have lost it. And when they saw that they were hemmed in between the caravel and the boats, they all hurled themselves into the sea, some seventy men perhaps, about two leagues from land; and pursuing them in the boats the entire day we were not able to take more than two of them, and them only by chance. All the others arrived safely ashore, and in the canoe they had left four boys not of their race, captives whom they were transporting from another land, and whom they had castrated, for they were all without their virile member and the wound was fresh: we marvelled greatly at this. After they were taken aboard the ships, they told us through signs that they had been castrated to be eaten; and then we knew that these were a very fierce people known as Cannibals, who eat human flesh.

We headed for the land with the boats, taking the canoe up with us over the stern, and anchored half a league from the shore. And since we saw many people on the beach, we headed for land in the boats and took with us the two men we had captured. And when we reached shore, everyone fled and took to the woods; and we sent ahead one of the men, giving him many bells and some mirrors, and we told him to reassure the people, and that we wanted to be their friends; which the man whom we sent did very well, bringing back with him all the people, which must have been four hundred men and many women, who came totally unarmed to where we were waiting with the boats. Having entered on friendly terms with them, we turned the other captive over to them and sent to the ships for their canoe and gave it back to them. This canoe was twenty-six paces long and two braccia wide, dug completely out of one tree, very well crafted; and once they had launched it onto a river and found it a safe place, they all fled and did not want to converse any further with us: which seemed such barbarous conduct that we judged them to be a people of little faith and poor condition. We noticed that some wore little bits of gold in their ears.

We departed thence and entered the bay, where we found so many people that it was a wonder, with whom we established complete friendship, and many of us went with them to their villages, in great safety and very well received. In this place we acquired 150 pearls, which they gave us for a bell, and a bit of gold, which they gave us as a gift. And in this land we found that they drank a wine which they made from fruits and seeds like beer, both white and red; and the best was made from myrobalans, and very good it was, and we ate an infinite number of these, since they were in season: it is a very good fruit, savory to the taste and healthy for the body. The land is very abundant in provisions, and people are pleasant in their converse and the most peaceful that we have encountered to this point.

We spent seventeen very pleasurable days in this port, and each day new people from the interior came to see us, marvelling at our features and whiteness and our clothing and weapons and the form and size of our ships. From this people we had news of a people to the west who were their enemies, who possessed an infinite quantity of pearls, which had belonged to them and been taken from them in their wars; and they told us how they had fished for them, and how they were formed, and we found that they were telling the truth, as Your Magnificence will hear.

We left this harbor, and sailed along the coast, on which we continually saw smoke and people on the beach, and after many days we came into a harbor in order to repair one of our ships which was taking in a great deal of water; there we found many people with whom we could not, by force or by love, establish any converse: and when we went to land with the boats, they fiercely barred our landing, and when they thwarted us no longer, they fled into the forests, and did not wait for us.

Recognizing how barbarous they were, we departed; and sailing on, we caught sight of an island fifteen leagues out at sea from the mainland; and we decided to go there and see if it was inhabited. We found there the most bestial people, and the ugliest we had ever seen, and this is what they were like: they were exceedingly ugly in face and demeanor, and they all had their cheeks stuffed with a green grass, which they chewed like beasts, so that they could barely speak; and each of them bore two small dried gourds around his neck, one filled with that grass which they kept in their mouth, and the other with a white flour which resembled powdered chalk: and every so often, having wetted with their mouth a certain spindle they carried, they put it in the gourd containing the flour, and then they would put it in their mouth on both sides of their cheeks, thus coating the weed they had in their mouth with the flour; and this they would do with great care. And astonished to see such a thing, we could not understand this secret, nor why they did it. This people, as soon as they saw us, approached us as familiarly as if we had long been their friends. Once we were going along the beach with them and talking, we were eager to drink some fresh water, but they made a sign to us that they had none, whereupon they offered us some of their grass and flour; so we deduced from their gestures that this island was poor in water, and that to quell their thirst they kept that grass in their mouths, and the flour for the same purpose.[36]

We went about the island for a day and a half without ever finding fresh water, and we saw that the water they drank was a dew which fell at night on certain leaves which looked like ass's ears, and which would fill up with water, and this was the water they drank (it was excellent); and these leaves did not grow in many places. These people had no foods or roots like those of the mainland, and they lived off the fish they caught in the sea, which they had in great abundance, and they were excellent fishermen; and they presented us with many tortoises, and many large and very good fish. Their women did not hold grass in their mouths like the men, but all carried a gourd with water from which they would drink. They had no villages with either houses or huts; rather they dwelt under branches which protected them from the sun and not from water, for I believe it rarely rained on that island. When they would fish on the sea, they all kept a very large leaf with them, so broad that they could stand beneath it in shade, and they would fix the same leaf into the ground, and, as the sun turned, so they would turn the leaf, and in this way they were protected from the sun. The island contains many animals of various sorts, which drink swamp water.

And seeing that they had nothing of value, we left, and came to another island, and found it inhabited by very large people. We went inland to see if we could find fresh water; and not thinking that the island was inhabited, since we had not seen people along the beach, we saw very large footprints of people in the sand, and judged that if their other limbs were proportional, they would be very large men. Continuing on, we came upon a path that headed inland, and nine of us decided, judging that the island, small as it was, could not have many people on it, to follow that path, and see what kind of people these were. And after we had travelled about a league, we saw five of their huts in a valley, which seemed abandoned; and we went up to them and found only five women—two old women and three girls—of such tall stature that we looked at them as at a wonder. And when they saw us, they were taken with such fear that they did not have the courage to flee; and the two old women started addressing words of hospitality to us, bringing us many things to eat, and taking us into a hut. And they were of taller stature than a tall man, as big in body as was Francesco degli Albizzi,[37] but better proportioned; so that we were all of a mind to take the three girls by force and carry them back to Castile as objects of wonder.

And while we were debating these matters, a full thirty-six men started to enter through the door of the hut, much bigger than the women, men so well built that they were a beautiful thing to behold; and these men threw us into such alarm that we would have much preferred to have been at the ships than to find ourselves with such people. They carried very big bows and arrows and large clubs with heads, and they spoke among themselves sounding as though they wanted to lay hands upon us. Seeing that we were in such danger, we debated various strategies among ourselves: some said it would be better to have at them there in the house, others said no, that it would be better to do so in the open field, and others proposed that we not set off hostilities until we understood their intentions; and we decided to leave the hut and head secretly for the path which led to the ships; and so we did, and, taking our path, we returned by it to the ships. But they followed behind us, at a stone's throw, talking among themselves: I believe they were as afraid of us as we were of them, because a few times we paused to rest and so did they, without coming closer to us; so that we reached the beach where the ships were waiting for us, and we boarded them. And when we were far from shore, they jumped into the water and shot many arrows at us, but by then we had little fear of them. We fired two shots of mortar at them, more to scare them than to harm them, and at the report they all fled into the woods; and so we left them, and it seemed to us that we had survived a most dangerous day. Like the others they went about completely naked. I call this island the Isle of Giants, because of their size.

We continued on, coasting along the land, during which we had many occasions to fight with them because they did not want to let us take anything from the land. We had already been of a mind to return from there to Castile, because we had been at sea about a year, and we had few provisions, and the few we had were damaged due to the great heat we had passed through, because, from the time we left the isles of Cape Verde to this point, we had sailed continuously through the Torrid Zone and twice over the equator, for, as I said above, we were five degrees beyond it to the south, and here we were fifteen degrees to the north;[38] once we had made this decision, it pleased the Holy Spirit to give some respite to our travails: for it happened that, in going in search of a port in which to repair our vessels, we encountered a people who received us most amiably; and we found that they had great quantities of oriental pearls, and quite fine ones. We stayed with these people for forty-seven days, and we acquired 119 marks of pearls for very little merchandise, which I do not think cost us even forty ducats, because we gave them nothing other than bells, mirrors and glass beads and brass leaves, for one of them traded all the pearls he had for one bell. We learned from them how they fished for them and where, and they gave us many oysters, in which pearls were hatched. We acquired an oyster in which 130 pearls were hatching, and others with less: the Queen took the one with 130 pearls from me, so I took care that she did not see any others. And Your Magnificence should know that, if the pearls do not mature and detach by themselves, they will not last, because they are easily damaged: and I have direct experience of this; when they are mature, they stay inside the oyster, detached and set into the flesh, and these are the good ones. The bad ones they had, for most were rough and badly punctured, were still worth good money, because each mark sold for sixty thousand [. . .].[39]

And after forty-seven days we left these people very much our friends. We departed, and went to purchase necessary provisions on the island of Antilia,[40] the one Chistopher Columbus discovered several years ago, where we bought many provisions and stayed two months and seventeen days; where we endured many dangers and labors with the Christians themselves who were on that island with Columbus—I believe it was from envy[41]—all of which, lest I lapse into prolixity, I shall leave untold. We departed from the said island on 22 July, and sailed for a month and a half, and entered the port of Cadiz on 8 September. We were well received, with honor and profit. Thus ended my second voyage, God be praised.

End of the second voyage.

The third begins.

I found myself thereafter in Seville, resting from the many travails which I had endured on these two voyages, and longing to return to the land of pearls, when fortune, not content with my travails—I do not know how the desire entered the mind of his Most Serene Highness King Don Manuel of Portugal to make use of me, and just when I was in Seville without one thought of going to Portugal, a messenger came to me with a letter from His Royal Crown, who requested me to come to Lisbon to speak with His

Highness, promising to show favor toward me. I was not inclined to go, and I dispatched the messenger, saying that I was ill and that when I had recovered, if His Highness still wished to make use of me, I would do his every bidding. And when he saw that he could not have me, he decided to send for me through Giuliano di Bartolomeo del Giocondo,[42] who was here in Lisbon, and had instructions to bring me back by whatever means. The said Giuliano came to Seville, and with his arrival and request I was forced to go there, which was looked upon with ill favor by all who knew me, because I left Castile, where I had won honor and was considered the rightful possession of the King; the worst was that I left without taking leave of my host.[43]

And when I presented myself before this King, he showed how pleased he was with my coming, and asked me to accompany three of his ships which stood ready to depart in search of new lands; and since the request of a king is a command, I had to accede to all he requested. And we left this port of Lisbon with three ships in convoy, on 10 May 1501, and took our course straight to Grand Canary Island, and without stopping passed within sight of it. And from there we coasted the shore of Africa on its western side, on which coast we made a catch of fish of the kind called porgies, and we remained there three days. And from there we went to the coast of Ethiopia, to a port called Bezeguiche,[44] which lies in the Torrid Zone, above which the North Pole rises 14½ degrees, located in the first climate; we stayed eleven days there, procuring water and firewood, because my intention was to sail southward across the waters of the Atlantic.

We left this port of Ethiopia and sailed on a course southwest by south, until, after sixty-seven days, we came upon a land which lay 700 leagues to the southwest of the said port. And during those sixty-seven days we withstood the worst weather any mariner has ever experienced, due to the many rains and storms and tempests brought our way, for we entered there at a very adverse time since the greater part of our sailing was always near the equator, which in the month of June is in winter. And we found the day and the night to be equal, and we always cast shadow to the south.

It pleased God to reveal new land to us on 17 August, where we anchored half a league from shore, and we lowered our boats, and went to see if the land was inhabited by people, and of what kind, and we found it to be inhabited by people who were worse than animals, and how this was so Your Magnificence will hear: at the outset we did not see people, yet we well knew that it was populated by many signs which we saw about the place. We took possession of it for this Most Serene King, and found it to be most pleasant and green land and of good appearance: it lay five degrees to the south of the equator. And the same day we returned to the ships.

And because we were in great need of water and firewood, we decided the next day to return to land to obtain the necessary provisions. And once ashore, we saw a tribe at the top of a mountain gazing down at us but did not dare to descend any lower: they were naked and of the same color and constitution as the others. And although we took great pains with them that they might come and speak with us, we could never reassure them, for they did not trust us; and since they were so persistent in this, and it was already late, we returned to the ships, leaving them many bells and mirrors and other things on the ground within their sight. And when we were far out at sea, they descended the mountain and came for the things which we had left them, over which they marvelled greatly. And that day we provisioned ourselves with nothing but water.

The next morning we saw from the ships that the people on land were sending up many clouds of smoke; and we, thinking that they were calling to us, made for shore, where we found that many people had come, though they kept their distance from us, and made signs to us that we should go with them into the interior. Whereupon two of our Christians were moved to ask the captain to give them permission to go, for they were willing to take the risk of going inland with them to see what kind of people they were and whether they had any wealth either of spices or of drugs; and they were so insistent that the captain acceded, and they equipped themselves with many items to trade. They left us, with instructions to return after no more than five days, which was as long as we could wait for them; and almost every day many new people came to the beach, yet never did they wish to speak with us.

And the seventh day we went ashore and found that they had brought their women with them; and when we landed, the men of the land sent many of their women to speak with us. And seeing that they were not reassured, we decided to send them one of our men, a youth who always showed much courage; and we, the better to reassure them, entered the boats, and he went to the women, and when he reached them, they gathered in a big circle around him: touching him and gazing upon him in admiration. As this was happening, we saw a woman come from the mountain, carrying a big club in her hand; and when she reached our Christian, she stole up from behind and, raising this club, gave him such a blow that it knocked him dead on the ground. And immediately the other women grabbed him by the feet and dragged him toward the mountain, and the men leaped toward the shore to shoot at us with their bows and arrows; and they so frightened our men, who were in the boats resting with the shallow-water anchors by the land, that despite all the many arrows they were shooting into the boats, no one managed to pick up his weapons. Yet we fired four charges of mortar at them, and while none of the shots hit anyone, the very sound of them was enough to send them fleeing toward the mountain, where the women were already hacking the Christian up into pieces, and, in a great fire they had built, were roasting him before our eyes, showing us many pieces and then eating them; and the men, indicating by their gestures that they had killed and eaten the other two Christians: which weighed upon us heavily, and we believed them, having seen with our our eyes the cruelties they committed upon the dead man. All of us considered this an intolerable wrong; and more than forty of us prepared to land and avenge such a beastly and cruel death, but the captain general would not consent; and they remained unpunished for so great an offense; we departed from them most unwillingly and greatly ashamed, because of our captain.

We left that place and began a new course east by southeast, for so trended the land; and we made many stops and never found people who wanted to parley with us. And sailing in this way we eventually found that the land turned to the southwest, and after doubling a cape, to which we gave the name of Cape San Augustín,[45] we began to sail to the southwest. And that cape lies 150 leagues to the east from the aforementioned land that we saw, where they killed the Christians; and the cape lies eight degrees south of the equator. And sailing one day, we had caught sight of many people standing on the beach to see the marvel of our ships; and since we were sailing in their direction, we went to them and anchored in a good spot, and went ashore in the boats, and found these people to be in a better state than the previous ones; and although it took much effort to tame them, we nevertheless made them our friends and traded with them. We stayed five days in this place, and here found very large *cassiafistula,* both fresh and dried, atop the trees. We decided to take a couple of men from this place to teach us their language, and three volunteered to come with us to Portugal.

And since I am already tired from so much writing, Your Magnificence will know that we departed from this harbor sailing always to the southwest within sight of land, continally making many stops and speaking with countless people. And we went so far south that we were already beyond the Tropic of Capricorn, where the South Pole rose 32 degrees above the horizon,[46] and we had already completely lost Ursa Minor, and Ursa Major was very low and appeared to us nearly at the edge of the horizon, and we guided ourselves by the stars of the South Pole, which are many and much larger and more luminous than those of our own pole. And I drew the figures of most of them, and especially of those of the first and greater magnitude, also identifying their orbits around the South Pole and their diameters and radii, as will be seen in my *Four Journeys*.

We ran along that coast for some 750 leagues: 150 to the west of the cape named after Saint Augustine, and 600 to the southwest; and if I desired to recount the things which I saw on that voyage and all that we underwent, I would need more new sheets than I have already written upon. And along this coast we saw nothing of value, except for infinitely many brazilwood trees, many cassia trees, and trees of the sort that produce courbaril, and so many other wonders of nature that they cannot be told.

Since we had already been ten months on the voyage, and since we had not found any sort of mineral in this land, we decided to leave it, and to go and try some other region in the sea. And holding counsel, we decided that we should follow that course which seemed best to me, and full command of the fleet was entrusted to me; and I then commanded that the entire crew and fleet be provisioned with water and firewood enough for six months, for such was the time the ships' officers had judged that we were capable of sailing with as much supply. Once we had obtained our provisions, we set out from this land and started our course to the southeast. It was 15 February; the sun was already approaching the equinox and returning toward our northern hemisphere. And we sailed by this wind until we found ourselves at such high latitude that the South Pole stood full 52 degrees above our horizon, and we saw the stars of neither Ursa Minor nor Ursa Major, and we were already five hundred leagues to the south of the harbor from which we had departed; and this was 3 April. And on this day a tempest began to rage so violently that we had to furl the sails completely and course on in the strong wind with bare masts, for these were southwesterly winds, with very high seas and the air very turbulent; and this storm was so fierce that the entire fleet was in great fear. The nights were very long, for we had a night on 7 April of fifteen hours, because the sun was at the end of Aries, making it winter in that region, as Your Magnificence may well reckon.

And sailing in this storm, we sighted new land[47] on 7 April, along which we ran some twenty leagues; and we found it to be all exposed coast, and we saw no harbor or people, I believe because the cold was so great, since no one in the fleet could either fend it off or bear it. Thus since we were in such danger, and in such a storm that we could scarcely discern one ship from another because of the high seas and the great darkness the storm created, we agreed with the captain general to signal the fleet that it should come together and that we should leave the land and set a course back to Portugal. And this was a very good decision, for it is certain that, had we lingered there that night, we would all have been lost, for no sooner had we turned the ships around, than the tempest so gathered in force that night and the next day that we thought we were lost; and we made vows to take pilgrimages,[48] and performed other ceremonies, as mariners are wont to do in such times.

We coursed on five days before the wind, with only the foresail, and that very low, and perhaps we sailed 250 leagues in those five days, yet all the while as we approached the equator the air and the seas grew more temperate; and it pleased God to deliver us from such grave danger. And our course lay betwen north and northeast, because it was our intention to go and reconnoiter the coast of Ethiopia, which lay one thousand three hundred leagues away, across the gulf of the Atlantic Sea; and with God's grace, on 10 May we arrived there, at a coastal land to the south, called Sierra Leone, where we spent fifteen days, restoring ourselves.

And from there we set off on a course toward the Azores Islands, which are about 750 leagues from this Sierra; and we sailed in among the islands at the end of July, staying there another fifteen days, taking some recreation. Whereupon we departed for Lisbon, from which we were three hundred leagues to the west, and we quite safely entered the Lisbon harbor on 7 September 1502 (thanks be to God), with only two ships, having burned the other one in Sierra Leone, because it was no longer seaworthy: for we had been on this voyage about sixteen months, and for eleven of those sailed without sight of the North Star, or Ursa Major or Minor (called the Horn), and guided ourselves by the stars of the other pole.

This is what I saw on this third voyage, or journey.

Fourth voyage.

It remains for me to relate the things which I saw on the fourth voyage, or journey; and since I am already tired, and also since this fourth voyage did not end as I had intended, due to a mishap that befell us in the gulf of the Atlantic Sea, as Your Magnificence will soon hear in the following, I shall strive to be brief.

We left this port of Lisbon in a convoy of six ships, intending to go and discover an island to the east called Malacca, which is reputed to be very rich, and is like a warehouse for all the ships that come from the Sea of the Ganges and the Indian Sea—just as Cadiz is storehouse for all the vessels which pass from east to west and from west to east—according to news which his Most Serene Highness the King has received by way of Calicut. And this Malacca lies farther to the west than Calicut, and much more to the south, for we know that it is situated 33 degrees[49] toward the Antarctic Pole.

We departed 10 May 1503 and headed for the Cape Verde Islands, where we procured our meat and all sorts of other fresh provisions, and where we spent thirteen days; and from there we set out upon our voyage, sailing a southeasterly course. And as our captain general was a presumptuous and very obstinate man, he chose to have us go reconnoiter Sierra Leone, a land of southern Ethiopia, for no good reason at all, except to show that he was captain of six ships, against the wishes of all us other captains. And while we thus were sailing, we reached that land, and so many were the storms, and so adverse the weather, that, although we were within sight of land four whole days, the bad weather never permitted us to take that land. So we were forced to return on our proper course and leave behind the aforementioned Sierra, and sailing thence on a south-southwest course, that is, south by southwest; and when we had sailed at least three hundred leagues over the monstrous expanse of the sea, and were already standing three degrees to the south of the equator, there appeared to us a land at a distance of about twenty-two leagues, and marvelous to behold. And we found that it was an island in the midst of the sea, and it was very high, truly a wonder of nature, because it was no more than two leagues long and one wide; no people had ever lived on this island. And it was the island of ill luck for the entire fleet, because Your Magnificence must know that, due to the bad judgement and guidance of our captain general, he lost his ship there, for he ran it up against a rock, and it was rent asunder the night of Saint Lawrence, which is 10 August, and it sank to the bottom, and nothing on it was saved except the crew. It was a ship of three hundred tons, and it held everything of importance to the fleet; and while the entire fleet struggled to save it, the captain commanded me to go with my ship to the said island to seek a good anchorage where we could anchor all the ships; and since my boat, loaded with nine of my sailors, was occupied with helping to lighten the ship, he did not want me to take it, and said that I should go without it, adding that they would take it to me at the island.

I parted from the fleet as he commanded me, heading to the island without a boat and with less than half of my sailors, and I arrived at the said island, about four leagues away. On this island I found a very good harbor, where all the ships could quite safely anchor; there for eight whole days I awaited my captain and the fleet, and they never came, which made us very unhappy. And the people who had remained with me on the ship were so afraid that I could not console them.

And in this situation, on the eighth day we saw a ship coming from the sea, and, fearing that it might not see us, we weighed anchor and went to her, thinking that it was bringing me my boat and crew. And as we came alongside it, after they hailed us, they told us that the captain's ship had sunk and that the crew had been saved, and that my boat and crew remained with the fleet, which had gone ahead on the sea: this was such grievous news for us, as Your Magnificence can imagine, since we found ourselves one thousand leagues from Lisbon, far out at sea with a small crew. Nonetheless we bore with fortune and nonetheless continued on.

We returned to the island and used the auxiliary boat in my convoy to supply ourselves with water and firewood; we found this island to be uninhabited, with many sources of fresh water and countless delightful trees, full of so many sea and land birds that they were without number, and were so guileless that they let themselves be taken in hand; and we took so many of them that we loaded a boat full of them. We did not see any animals, except for very large rats, green lizards with two tails, and some snakes.

Having provisioned ourselves, we departed on a course south by southwest, because we had an order from the king commanding that, should any ship lose its fleet or the captain, it should head toward the land that we discovered on the last voyage, to a port that we had named the Bay of All Saints.[50] And it pleased God to give us such good weather that in seventeen days we arrived there—it lay a full three hundred leagues from the island—where we found neither our captain nor any other ship in the fleet; in this port we waited a full two months and four days.

And since no word arrived, the convoy ship and I decided to run the coast, and we sailed ahead 260 leagues, until we reached a harbor where we decided to build a fort; and build it we did, and left there twenty-four Christian men whom my convoy had picked up from the captain's ship that had been lost. We remained five whole months in that harbor, building the fort and loading our ships with brazilwood, for we could not go on ahead because we did not have the crew and I lacked much equipment. Having done all this, we decided to return to Portugal, which was on a course northeast by north; and we left behind twenty-four men to remain in the fort, supplies for six months, twelve mortars and many other weapons; and we pacified all the people of that land, of whom no mention has been made for this voyage, but not because we did not see and have dealings with countless people there: for thirty of our men went forty leagues inland, where I myself saw so many things I must delay relating, saving them for my *Four Journeys*. This land lies eighteen degrees to the south of the equator, 37 degrees to the west of the meridian of Lisbon, according to what our instruments showed.

And once we had done all this, we left the Christians and that land, and started on our course to the north-northeast, that is, the course north by northeast, intending to travel directly on that course to this city of Lisbon. And seventy-seven days later, after so many hardships and dangers, we arrived in this harbor on 18 June 1504, God be praised; here we were very well received, and unbelievably so, for the whole city had given us up for lost, since all the other ships in the fleet had been lost through the pride and folly of our captain, for thus God does reward pride. And at present I find myself here, in Lisbon, and do not know what the King intends for me, though I very much desire rest.

The present message-bearer, Benvenuto di Domenico Benvenuti, will tell Your Magnificence of my situation and of some things which I left unsaid to avoid prolixity, for he has seen and heard them. God be with him.

Lord, I have shortened the letter as much as I could, and left unspoken many remarkable things in order not to be prolix. May Your Magnificence pardon me, I pray that you will count me among your servants; and I recommend to you Ser Antonio Vespucci, my brother,[51] and all my house.

I am left praying to God that he lengthen the days of your life, and exalt the state of that sublime Republic and the honor of Your Magnificence, etc.

Entrusted in Lisbon, on 4 September 1504.

By Your Magnificence's
humble servant
Amerigo Vespucci, in Lisbon

APPENDICES

APPENDIX A

LETTER FROM THE ADMIRAL CHRISTOPHER
COLUMBUS TO HIS SON, REFERRING TO
AMERIGO VESPUCCI.[1]

My Dear Son,—Diego Mendez left here on Monday, the 3rd of this month. After his departure, I spoke with Amerigo Vespucci, the bearer of this letter, who is going to the Court on matters relating to navigation. He always showed a desire to please me, and is a very respectable man. Fortune has been adverse to him, as to many others. His labours have not been so profitable to him as he might have expected. He leaves me with the desire to do me service, if it should be in his power. I am unable here to point out in what way he could be useful to me, because I do not know what may be required at Court; but he goes with the determination of doing all he can for me. You will see in what way he can be employed. Think the matter over, as he will do everything, and speak, and put things in train; but let all be done secretely, so as not to arouse suspicion of him. I have told him all I can about my affairs, and of the payments that have been made to me and are due. This letter is also for the Adelantado, for he can see in what way use can be made of it, and will apprise you of it, etc., etc.

Dated in Seville, the 5th of February (1505).

S.
S. A. S.
X. M. Y.
XPO FERENS.

APPENDIX B

ROYAL LETTER OF NATURALIZATION IN THE KINGDOMS OF CASTILLE AND LEON IN FAVOUR OF VESPUCCI[2]

As the letter from Columbus to his son Diego (5 Feb. 1505) documents, in this same month Vespucci was summoned to the court in the city of Toro to discuss "matters relating to navigation" (in this specific case, to take on the task of equipping a ship, for which the navigator received, the following 11 April, an advance of 12,000 maravedís). Vespucci thus was officially reentering the service of Spain, which was obviously interested in making use of the experience he had acquired in previous voyages, above all the Portuguese voyage of 1501-1502, which was a quest to find the southwest passage. It is for this reason that the navigator was accorded Spanish citizenship, in view of his loyalty and for past and, it was hoped, future services: an act which, for the foreigner Vespucci, was primarily a guarantee of political protection and of public commissions. What we have here is the related decree, issued in the city of Toro by Joan of Castile, and now in the General Archive of Simancas.

Doña Juana by the Grace of God:—To do good and show grace to you, Amerigo Vespucci, Florentine, in recognition of your fidelity and of certain good service you have done, and which I expect that you will do from henceforward, by this present I make you a native of these my kingdoms of Castille and of Leon, and that you may be able to hold any public offices that you may have been given or charged with, and that you may be able to enjoy and may enjoy all the honours, favours, and liberties, pre-eminences, prerogatives and immunities, and all other things, and each one of them, which you would be able or would be bound to have and enjoy if you were born in these kingdoms and lordships.

By this my letter, and by its duplicate signed by a public notary, I order the most illustrious Prince Don Carlos, my very dear and well-beloved son, and the Infants, Dukes, Prelates, Counts, Marquises, Ricos-Hombres, Masters of the Orders, those of my Council, the judges of my courts, the magistrates of my house and court, the friars, commanders and sub-commanders of the orders, governors of castles and forts, the councillors, governors, assistant-governors, officers, knights, esquires, and citizens of all my cities, towns, and villages of these my kingdoms and lordships, and all others my subjects, of whatsoever condition, pre-eminence, or dignity they be or may be, that they shall consider you as a native of these my kingdoms and lordships, as if you had been born and brought up in them, and leave you to hold such public and royal offices and posts as may be given and entrusted to you, and such other things as you shall have an interest in, the same as if you had been born and bred in these kingdoms; and they shall maintain and cause to maintain the said honours, favours, freedoms, liberties, exemptions, pre-eminences, prerogatives and immunities, and all other things, and each one of them, that you may or ought to have and enjoy, being native of these the said my kingdoms and lordships, and that neither on them nor on any part of them shall they place, or consent to be placed, any impediment against you.

Thus I order that it shall be done, any laws or ordinances of these my kingdoms to the contrary notwithstanding, as to which or to each of them of my proper motion and certain knowledge, and absolute royal power, such as I choose to use as Queen and Natural Lady of this part, I dispense so far as they touch these presents, leaving them in force and vigour for all other things henceforward.

Given in the city of Toro, on the 24th day of April, in the year of the birth of our Lord Jesus Christ, 1505 years. I, the King.

I, Gaspar de Goicio. Licentiate Zapata. Licenciate Polanco.

APPENDIX C

APPOINTMENT OF AMERIGO VESPUCCI
AS CHIEF PILOT

The year 1505 marks a resurgence of colonization in the area of the Antilles, the oldest of discovered lands; an associate of Vespucci, the Florentine Giannotto Berardi, had already addressed a Memorial *on this subject to Isabella of Castile in 1495. A colonizing venture, part private and part public, was actively underway, organized by Vicente Yáñez Pinzón and Amerigo Vespucci, with sharing of expenses and profits by Ferdinand the Catholic. This explains Amerigo's being summoned to the court in November and February 1507, in the company of Juan de la Cosa, Vicente Yáñez Pinzón, and Juan Díaz de Solís. It also explains Vespucci's appointment as* Piloto Mayor, *which took place 22 March 1508 and was confirmed on the following 6 August with the royal decree issued, in name of Joan of Castile, in the city of Valladolid. The appointment required him to set up a school, and to do so* ad personam *(and the decree for this institution and for the appointment in fact coincide), for the purpose of improving the technical level of the Spanish navy assigned to ocean routes; a decision prompted by the frequency of accidents on the high seas (primarily shipwrecks), which gravely compromised the safety of ships and cargo. The "Chief Pilot" was expected, in fact, to select, train, and examine future "pilots," in addition to supervising technical equipment and steadily providing information to the* Padrón Real: *the general and official map of discovered lands had to be a unitary composite of the partial maps the captains, on their return to Spain, were required to submit to officials of the Casa de la Contratación. In this way the crown managed to guarantee itself the monopoly on the discovery, reducing the participatory role of the private concerns, while for Vespucci it meant the official recognition of his nautical and cartographical expertise. Amerigo's school was private, even down to the protective clause that instruction be open to "whosoever should desire and be able to pay the agreed-upon fee." The theoretical lessons took place in the home of the navigator, who was assisted by a "piloto real," in the person of Juan Díaz de Solís, Vespucci's eventual successor as "Chief Pilot," while the role of "piloto real" went to Giovanni Vespucci (also see introduction p. xxxvii).*

Doña Juana:—Seeing that it has come to our notice, and that we have seen by experience, that, owing to the pilots not being so expert as is necessary, nor so well instructed in what they ought to know, so as to be competent to rule and govern the ships that navigate in the voyage over the Ocean Sea to our islands and mainland which we possess in the Indies; and that through their default, either in not knowing how to rule and govern, or through not knowing how to find the altitude by the quadrant or astrolabe, nor the methods of calculating it, have happened many disasters, and those who have sailed under their governance have been exposed to great danger, by which our Lord has been ill-served, as well as our finances, while the merchants who trade thither have received much hurt and loss. And for a remedy to the above, and because it is necessary as well for that navigation as for other voyages by which, with the help of our Lord, we hope to make new discoveries in other lands, that there should be persons who are more expert and better instructed, and who know the things necessary for such navigation, so that those who are under them may go more safely, it is our will and pleasure, and we order that all the pilots of our kingdoms and lordships, who are now or shall hereafter be appointed as pilots in the said navigation to the islands and mainland that we possess in the parts of the Indies, and in other parts of the Ocean Sea, shall be instructed and shall know what it is necessary for them to know respecting the quadrant and astrolabe, in order that, by uniting theory with practice, they may be able to make good use of them in the said voyages made to the said parts, and, without such knowledge, no one shall go in the said ships as pilots, nor receive pay as pilots, nor may the masters receive them on board ship, until they have first been examined by you, Amerigo Despuchi, our Chief Pilot, and they shall be given by you a certificate of examination and approval touching the knowledge of each one. Holding the said certificates, we order that they shall be taken and received as expert pilots by whoever is shown them, for it is our pleasure that you shall be examiner of the said pilots.

In order that those who have not the knowledge may more easily learn, we order that you are to teach them, in your house in Seville, all those things that they ought to know, you receiving payment for your trouble. And as it may happen that now, in the beginning, there may be a scarcity of passed pilots, and some ships may be detained for the want of them, causing loss and harm to the citizens of the said islands, as well as to merchants and other persons who trade thither, we order you, the said Amerigo, and we give you licence that you may select the most efficient pilots from among those who have been there, that for one or two voyages, or for a certain period, they may supply what is necessary, while those others acquire the knowledge that they have to learn, so that there may be time for them to learn what is needed.

It is also reported to us that there are many charts, by different masters, on which are delineated the lands and islands of the

Indies to us belonging, which by our order have recently been discovered, and that these charts differ very much one from another, as well in the routes as in the delineations of coasts, which may cause much inconvenience. In order that there may be uniformity, it is our pleasure, and we order that there shall be made a general chart (*Padrón General*), and that it may be more accurate, we order our officers of the House of *Contratación* at Seville that they shall assemble all the ablest pilots that are to be found in the country at the time, and that, in the presence of you, Amerigo Despuchi, our Chief Pilot, a padrón of all the lands and islands of the Indies that have hitherto been discovered belonging to our kingdoms and lordships shall be made; and that for it, after consulting and reasoning with those pilots, and in accord with you, the said Chief Pilot, a general *padrón* shall be constructed, which shall be called the *Padrón Real*, by which all pilots shall be ruled and governed, and that it shall be in the possession of the aforesaid our officers, and of you, our Chief Pilot; and that no pilot shall use any other chart, but only one which has been taken from the *Padrón Real*, on pain of a fine of fifty *dobles* towards the works of the House of *Contratación* of the Indies in the city of Seville.

We further order all the pilots of our kingdoms and lordships who, from this time forward, shall go to the said our lands of the Indies, discovered or to be discovered, that, when they find new lands, islands, bays, or harbours, or anything else, that they make a note of them for the said *Padrón Real*, and on arriving in Castille that they shall give an account to you, the said our Chief Pilot, and to the officers of the House of *Contratación* of Seville, that all may be delineated properly on the said *Padrón Real*, with the object that navigators may be better taught and made expert in navigation. We further order that none of our pilots who navigate the

Ocean Sea, from this time forward, shall go without their quadrant and astrolabe and the rules for working them, under the penalty that those who do not comply be rendered incompetent to exercise the said employment during our pleasure, and they shall not resume such employment without our special licence, paying a fine of 10,000 maravedís towards the works of the said House of *Contratación* at Seville. Amerigo Despuchi shall use and exercise the said office of our Chief Pilot, and you are empowered to do so, and you shall do all the things contained in this letter, and which appertain to the said office; and by this our letter, and by its copy attested by the public notary, we order the Prince Charles, our very dear and well-beloved son, the Infantes, Dukes, Prelates, Counts, Marquises, Ricos-hombres, Masters or Orders, Members of Council, and Judges of our Courts and Chancelleries, and the other priors, commanders, subcommanders, castellans of our castles and forts, the magistrates, officers of justice, knights, esquires, officers, and good men of all the cities, towns, and villages of our kingdoms and lordships, and all captains of ships, master mariners, pilots, mates, and all other persons whom our letter concerns or may concern, that you have and hold as our Chief Pilot, and consent and allow him to hold the said office, and to do and comply with all the things in this our letter or appertaining to it, and for their accomplishment and execution give all the favour and help that is needful for all that is here, and for each part of it; and that the above may come to the knowledge of all, and that none may pretend ignorance, we order that this our letter shall be read before the public notary, in the markets and open spaces, and other accustomed places in the said city of Seville, and in the city of Cadiz, and in all the other cities, towns, and villages of these kingdoms and lordships; and if hereafter any person or persons act against it, the said justices shall execute upon them the penalties contained in this letter, so that the above shall be observed and shall take effect without fail; and if the one or the others do not so comply, they shall be subject to a fine of 10,000 maravedís for our chamber. Further we order the man to whom this letter shall be shown, that he shall appear before us in our Court, wherever we may be for fifteen following days under the said penalty, for which we order whatever public notary may be called for this, shall give testimony signed with his seal, that we may know that our order has been executed.

Given in the city of Valladolid, the 6th of August, in the year of the birth of the Lord Jesus Christ, 1508. I, the King.

I, Lope Cunchillos, Secretary to the Queen our Lady, caused this to be written by order of the King her father. Witnessed: The Bishop of Palencia; Licentiate Ximenes.

APPENDIX D

From Martin Waldseemüller's
COSMOGRAPHIAE INTRODUCTIO

PREFACE
TO HIS MAJESTY
MAXIMILIAN CÆSAR AUGUSTUS
MARTINUS ILACOMILUS WISHES GOOD FORTUNE

On 25 April 1507, at Saint-Dié of Lorraine, a Cosmographiae
Introductio *was published, edited by the cosmographer Martin
Waldseemüller (Latinized as Hylacomilus, 1470-1518), who drew
on the collaboration of a group of scholars from the local* Gymnase
Vosgien, *under the protection of René II, Duke of Lorraine and Bar
and nominal King of Sicily and Jerusalem. The work aimed to
update Ptolemaic geography by means of the latest geographical
findings, to which end Waldseemüller decided to include a Latin
translation of Vespucci's letter to Piero Soderini (*Quattuor Americi Vesputii Navigationes), *made expressly for this work by Jean
Basin de Sendacour (Latinized as Johannes Basinus Sendacurius).
The manual, which contains a dedication of the cosmographer
Mathias Ringman (Philesius Vogesigena) to the Emperor Maximilian of Austria, was accompanied by a planisphere, a nautical map,
and a globe charting the known lands together with those discovered between the end of the fifteenth and beginning of the sixteenth
century; it is here that for the first time the name* America *is
attributed to the South American continent, in keeping with a
suggestion made and amply justified in the same treatise (for an
illustration, cf. Harley 1990, pp. 66 and 67).*

If it is not only pleasant but also profitable in life to visit many lands and to see the most distant races (a fact that is made clear in Plato, Apollonius of Tyana, and many other philosophers, who went to the most remote regions for the purpose of exploration), who, I ask, most invincible Maximilian Cæsar, will deny that it is pleasant and profitable to learn from books the location of lands and cities and of foreign peoples,

> Which Phoebus sees when he buries his rays
>   beneath the waves,
> Which he sees as he comes from the farthest east,
> Which the cold northern stars distress,
> Which the south wind parches with its torrid heat,
> Baking again the burning sands?
> *Boethius.*

Who, I repeat, will deny that it is pleasant and profitable to learn from books the manners and customs of all these peoples? Surely—to express my own opinion—just as it is worthy of praise to travel far, so it can not be foolish for one who knows the world, even from maps alone, to repeat again and again that passage of the Odyssey which Homer, the most learned of poets, wrote about Ulysses:

> Tell me, O Muse, of the man who after the
> capture of Troy
> Saw the customs and the cities of many men.

Therefore, studying, to the best of my ability and with the aid of several persons, the books of Ptolemy from a Greek copy, and adding the relations of the four voyages of Amerigo Vespucci, I have prepared for the general use of scholars a map of the whole world—like an introduction, so to speak—both in the solid and projected on the plane. This work I have determined to dedicate to your most sacred Majesty, since you are the lord of the world, feeling certain that I shall accomplish my end and shall be safe from the intrigues of my enemies under your protecting shield, as though under that of Achilles, if I know that I have satisfied, to some extent at least, your Majesty's keen judgment in such matters. Farewell, most illustrious Cæsar.

At St. Dié, in the year 1507 after the birth of Our Saviour.

CHAPTER IX
Of Certain Elements of Cosmography

It is clear from astronomical demonstrations that the whole earth is a point in comparison with the entire extent of the heavens; so that if the earth's circumference be compared to the size of the celestial globe, it may be considered to have absolutely no extent. There is about a fourth part of this small region in the world which was known to Ptolemy and is inhabited by living beings like ourselves. Hitherto it has been divided into three parts, Europe, Africa, and Asia.

Europe is bounded on the west by the Atlantic Ocean, on the north by the British Ocean, on the east by the river Tanais (modern Don), Lake Maeotis (modern Sea of Azov), and the Black Sea, and on the south by the Mediterranean Sea. It includes Spain, Gaul, Germany, Rætia, Italy, Greece, and Sarmatia. Europe is so called after Europa, the daughter of King Agenor. While with a girl's enthusiasm she was playing on the sea-shore accompanied by her Tyrian maidens and was gathering flowers in baskets, she is believed to have been carried off by Jupiter, who assumed the form of a snow-white bull, and after being brought over the seas to Crete seated upon his back to have given her name to the land lying opposite.

Africa is bounded on the west by the Atlantic Ocean, on the south by the Ethiopian Ocean, on the north by the Mediterranean Sea, and on the east by the river Nile. It embraces the Mauritanias, viz., Tingitana (modern Tangiers) and Cæsarea, inland Libya, Numidia (also called Mapalia), lesser Africa (in which is Carthage, formerly the constant rival of the Roman empire), Cyrenaica, Marmarica (modern Barca), Libya (by which name also the whole of Africa is called, from Libs, a king of Mauritania), inland Ethiopia, Egypt, etc. It is called Africa because it is free from the severity of the cold.

Asia, which far surpasses the other divisions in size and in resources, is separated from Europe by the river Tanais (Don) and from Africa by the Isthmus, which stretching southward divides the Arabian and the Egyptian seas. The principal countries of Asia are Bithynia, Galatia, Cappadocia, Pamphylia, Lydia, Cilicia, greater and lesser Armenia, Colchis, Hyrcania, Iberia, and Albania; besides many other countries which it would only delay us to enumerate one by one. Asia is so called after a queen of that name.

Now, these parts of the earth have been more extensively explored and a fourth part has been discovered by Amerigo Vespucci (as will be set forth in what follows). Inasmuch as both Europe and Asia received their names from women, I see no reason why any one should justly object to calling this part Amerige, i.e., the land of Amerigo, or America, after Amerigo, its discoverer, a man of great ability. Its position and the customs of

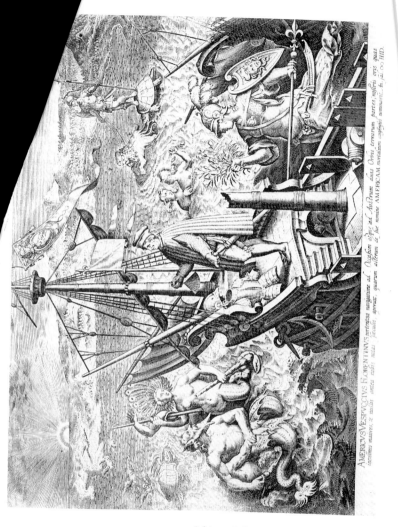

Adriaen Collaert, after Joannes Stradanus,
"Vespucci's Voyage of Discovery," 1497, issued ca. 1585.
*I.N. Phelps Stokes Collection, Miriam and Ira Wallach Division of Art, Prints and
Photographs, The New York Public Library; Astor, Lenox and Tilden Foundations*

its inhabitants may be clearly understood from the four voyages of
Amerigo, which are subjoined.

Thus the earth is now known to be divided into four parts. The
first three parts are continents, while the fourth is an island,
inasmuch as it is found to be surrounded on all sides by the ocean.
Although there is only one ocean, just as there is only one earth,
yet, being marked by many seas and filled with numberless
islands, it takes various names. These names may be found in the
Cosmography, and Priscian in his translation of Dionysius enu-
merates them in the following lines:

"The vast abyss of the ocean, however, surrounds the earth on
every side; but the ocean, although there is only one, takes many
names. In the western countries it is called the Atlantic Ocean,
but in the north, where the Arimaspi are ever warring, it is called
the sluggish sea, the Saturnian Sea, and by others the Dead
Sea, . . .

"Where, however, the sun rises with its first light, they call it
the Eastern or the Indian Sea. But where the inclined pole
receives the burning south wind, it is called the Ethiopian or the
Red sea, . . .

"Thus, the great ocean, known under various names, encircles
the whole world; . . .

"Of its arms the first that stretches out breaks through Spain
with its waves, and extends from the shores of Libya to the coast
of Pamphylia. This is smaller than the rest. A larger gulf is the one
that enters into the Caspian land, which receives it from the vast
waters of the north. The arm of the sea which Tethys (the ocean)
rules as the Saturnian Sea is called the Caspian or the Hyrcanian.
But of the two gulfs that come from the south sea, one, the
Persian, running northward, forms a deep sea, lying opposite the

country where the Caspian waves roll; while the other rolls and beats the shores of Panchæa and extends to the south opposite to the Euxine Sea. . . .

"Let us begin in regular order with the waters of the Atlantic, which Cadiz makes famous by Hercules' gift of the pillar, where Atlas, standing on a mountain, holds up the columns that support the heavens. The first sea is the Iberian, which separates Europe from Libya, washing the shores of both. On either side are the pillars. Both face the shores, the one looking toward Libya, the other toward Europe. Then comes the Gallic Sea, which beats the Celtic shores. After this the sea, called by the name of the Ligurians, where the masters of the world grew up on Latin soil, extends from the north to Leucopetra; where the island of Sicily with its curving shore forms a strait. Cyrnos (modern Corsica) is washed by the waters that bear its name and flow between the Sardinian Sea and the Celtic. Then rolls the surging tide of the Tyrrhenian Sea, turning toward the south; it enters the sea of Sicily, which turns toward the east and spreading far from the shores of Pachynum extends to Crete, a steep rock, which stands out of the sea, where powerful Gortyna and Phæstum are situated in the midst of the fields. This rock, resembling with its peak the forehead of a ram, the Greeks have justly called Κριοῦ μέτωπον (ram's forehead). The sea of Sicily ends at Mt. Garganus on the coast of Apulia.

"Beginning there the vast Adriatic extends toward the northwest. There also is the Ionian Sea, famous throughout the world. It separates two shores, which, however, meet in one point. On the right fertile Illyria extends, and next to this the land of the warlike Dalmatians. But its left is bounded by the Ausonian peninsula, whose curving shores the three seas, the Tyrrhenian,

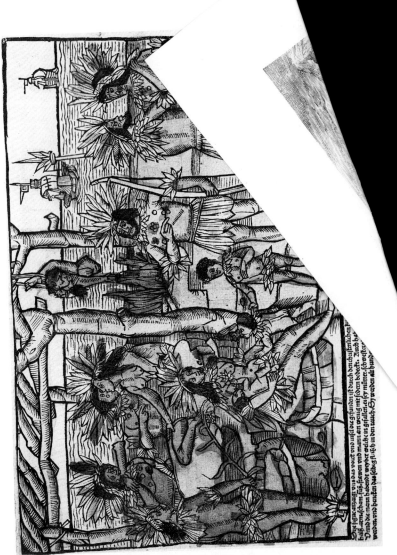

Anonymous, early German woodcut of a New World scene, ca. 1505.
Spencer Collection, The New York Public Library
Astor, Lenox and Tilden Foundations

Theodor Galle, after Joannes Stradanus,
"Vespucci Discovering America," from NOVA REPERTA.
Print Collection, Miriam and Ira D. Wallach Division of Art, Prints and Photographs, The New York Public Library; Astor, Lenox and Tilden Foundations

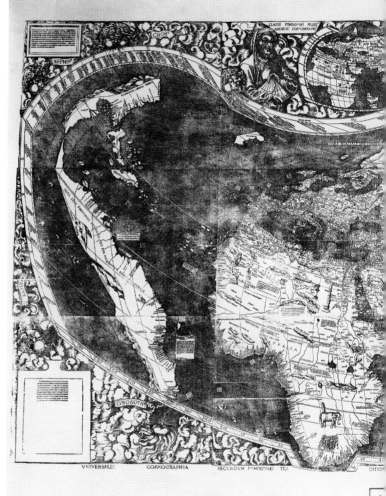

World Map, from Martin Waldseemüller,
COSMOGRAPHIAE INTRODUCTIO, St. Dié, 1507.
*Rare Books and Manuscript Division, The New York Public Library
Astor, Lenox and Tilden Foundations*

Detail from Martin Waldseemüller's World Map

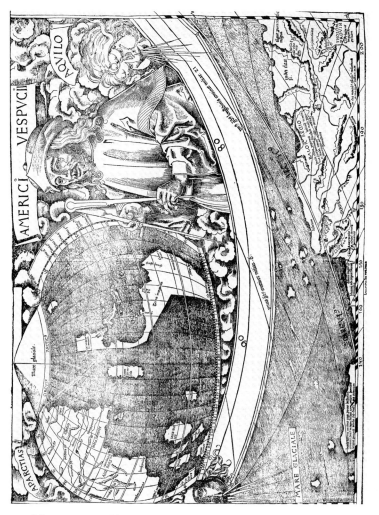

Detail from Martin Waldseemüller's World Map

Vespucci, MUNDUS NOVUS, Augsburg, 1504.
*Rare Books and Manuscript Division, The New York Public Library
Astor, Lenox and Tilden Foundations*

the Sicilian, and the vast Adriatic, encircle on all sides. Each of these seas within its limits has a wind peculiar to itself. The west wind lashes the Tyrrhenian, the south wind the Sicilian, while the east wind breaks the waters of the Adriatic which roll beneath its blasts.

"Leaving Sicily the sea spreads its deep expanse to the greater Syrtis which the coast of Libya encircles. After the greater Syrtis passes into the lesser, the two seas beat far and wide upon the re-echoing shores. From Sicily the Cretan Sea stretches out toward the east as far as Salmonis, which is said to be the eastern end of Crete.

"Next come two vast seas with dark waves, lashed by the north wind coming from Ismarus, which rushes straight down from the regions of the north. The first, called the Pharian Sea, washes the base of a steep mountain. The second is the Sidonian Sea, which turns toward the north, where the gulf of Issus joins it. This sea does not continue far in a straight line; for it is broken by the shores of Cilicia. Then bending westward it winds like a dragon because, forcing its way through the mountains, it devastates the hills and worries the forests. Its end bounds Pamphylia and surrounds the Chelidonian rocks. Far off to the west it ends near the heights of Patara.

"Next look again toward the north and behold the Ægean Sea, whose waves exceed those of all other seas, and whose vast waters surround the scattered Cyclades. It ends near Imbros and Tenedos, near the narrow strait through which the waters of the Propontis issue, beyond which Asia with its great peoples extends to the south, where the wide peninsula stretches out. Then comes the Thracian Bosporus, the mouth of the Black Sea. In the whole world they say there is no strait narrower than this. There are found the Symplegades, close together. There to the east the

Black Sea spreads out, situated in a northeasterly direction. From either side a promontory stands out in the middle of the waters; one, coming from Asia on the south, is called Carambis; the other on the opposite side juts out from the confines of Europe and is called Κριοῦ μέτωπον (ram's forehead). They face each other, therefore, separated by a sea so wide that a ship can cross it only in three days. Thus you may see the Black Sea looking like a double sea, resembling the curve of a bow, which is bent when the string is drawn tight. The right side resembles the string, for it forms a straight line, outside of which line is found Carambis only, which projects toward the north. But the coast that encloses the sea on the left side, making two turns, describes the arc of the bow. Into this sea toward the north Lake Mæotis (modern Sea of Azov) enters, enclosed on all sides by the land of the Scythians, who call Lake Mæotis the mother of the Black Sea. Indeed, here the violent sea bursts forth in a great stream, rushing across the Cimmerian Bosporus (modern Crimea), in those cold regions where the Cimmerians dwell at the foot of Taurus. Such is the picture of the ocean; such the glittering appearance of the deep."
(Priscian, Periegesis, 37, foll., ed. of Krehl.)

The sea, as we have said before, is full of islands, of which the largest and the most important, according to Ptolemy, are the following:

Taprobane (modern Ceylon), in the Indian Ocean under the equator; Albion, also called Britain and England; Sardinia, in the Mediterranean Sea; Candia, also called Crete, in the Ægean Sea; Selandia; Sicily, in the Mediterranean Sea; Corsica, Cyprus.

Unknown to Ptolemy: Madagascar, in the Prasodes Sea; Zanzibar; Java, in the East Indian Ocean; Angama; Peuta, in the Indian Ocean; Seula; Zipangri (Japan), in the Western Ocean.

Of these Priscian says:

"These are the large islands which the waters of the ocean surround. There are many other smaller islands, scattered about in different parts of the world, that are unknown, and that are either difficult of access to hardy sailors or suitable for harbors. Their names I cannot easily express in verse."
Periegesis, 609-613.

In order to be able to find out the distance between one place and another, the elevation of the pole must first be considered. It should therefore be briefly remarked that, as is clear from what precedes, both poles are on the horizon for those who live on the parallel of the equator. But as one goes toward the north, the elevation of the pole increases the farther one goes away from the equator. This elevation of the pole indicates the distance of places from the equator. For the distance of any place from the equator varies as the elevation of the pole at that place. From this the number of miles is easily ascertained, if you will multiply the number of degrees of elevation of the pole. But according to Ptolemy, from the equator to the arctic pole miles are not equal in all parts of the world. For any one of the degrees from the first degree of the equator up to the twelfth contains sixty Italian miles, which are equivalent to fifteen German miles, four Italian miles being generally reckoned equal to one German mile. Any degree from the twelfth degree up to the twenty-fifth contains fifty-nine miles, or fourteen and three-quarter German miles.

In order to make the matter clearer, we shall insert the following table:

	Degrees	Degrees	Italian Miles	German Miles
Equator	1 up to	12 cont'ng	60	15
	12	25	59	14 ¾
Tropic	25	30	54	13 ½
	30	37	50	12 ½
	37	41	47	11 ¼*
	51	57	32	8
	57	63	28	7
	63	66	26	6 ½
Arctic Circle	66	70	21	5 ¼
	70	80	6	1 ½
Arctic Pole	80	90		0

*Error for 11 ¼.

In like manner from the equator to either arctic or antarctic pole the number of miles in a degree of latitude varies. If you wish to find out the number of miles between one place and another, examine carefully in what degree of latitude the two places are and how many degrees there are between them; then find out from the above table how many miles there are in a degree of that kind, and multiply this number by the number of degrees between the places. The result will be the number of miles between them. Since these will be Italian miles, divide by four and you will have German miles.

All that has been said by way of introduction to the Cosmography will be sufficient, if we merely advise you that in designing the sheets of our world-map we have not followed Ptolemy in every respect, particularly as regards the new lands, where on the marine charts we observe that the equator is placed otherwise than Ptolemy represented it. Therefore those who notice this ought not to find fault with us, for we have done so purposely, because in this we have followed Ptolemy, and elsewhere the marine charts. Ptolemy himself, in the fifth chapter of his first book, says that he was not acquainted with all parts of the continent on account of its great size, that the position of some parts on account of the carelessness of travelers was not correctly handed down to him, and that there are other parts which happen at different times to have undergone variations on account of the cataclysms or changes in consequence of which they are known to have been partly broken up. It has been necessary therefore, as he himself says he also had to do, to pay more attention to the information gathered in our own times. We have therefore arranged matters so that in the plane projection we have followed Ptolemy as regards the new lands and some other things, while on the globe, which accompanies the plane, we have followed the description of Amerigo that we subjoin.

APPENDIX E

LAS CASAS ON THE
ALLEGED FIRST VOYAGE OF AMERIGO VESPUCCI.

In Book I of the Historia general de las Indias *(published in 1875), the Dominican Bartolomé de Las Casas (Seville, 1474, Madrid, 1566) launches a slander campaign against Vespucci, who he claims was guilty of stealing the glory from Columbus, for whom the Continent should have been named. The charge was later repeated by Antonio de Herrera y Tordesillas (1550-1615), author of a* Historia general de los hechos de los Castellanos en las islas y tierra firme del Mar Océano, *Madrid, 1601-1615. Needless to say, there was an ulterior motive to the charge Las Casas raised, which fits in with the legal action Columbus's heirs took against the Fiscal; the Dominican was in fact a great admirer of the Admiral (paraphrasing in its entirety the* Diario de a bordo *of the first voyage), while he is known to have had relations with the Colón family, and in particular with Don Fernando. Be that as it may, it must be said in defense of the friar that he had no knowledge of the actual turn of events, specifically the fact that it was not Vespucci himself, but Martin Waldseemüller, who was responsible for the eponym (cf. the present pp. 113 ff.). Moreover, it must be noted that Las Casas had only one source: the letter to Piero Soderini, which he knew in the Latin version of 1507, and whose authenticity he had no reason to doubt.*

CHAPTER CXL

It is manifest that the Admiral Don Cristóbal Colón was the first by whom Divine Providence ordained that this our great continent should be discovered, and chose him for the instrument through whom all these hitherto unknown Indies should be shown to the world. He saw it on Wednesday, the 1st of August, one day after he discovered the island of Trinidad, in the year of our salvation, 1498.[3] He gave it the name of Isla Santa, believing that it was an island. He then began to enter the Gulf of La Bellena, by the entrance called the mouth of the Serpent by him, finding all the water fresh, and it is this entrance which forms the island of Trinidad, separating it from the mainland called Santa. On the following Friday, being the 3rd of August, he discovered the point of Paria, which he also believed to be an island, giving it the name of Gracia. But all was mainland, as in due time appeared, and still more clearly now is it known that here there is an immense continent.

It is well here to consider the injury and injustice which that Americo Vespucio appears to have done to the Admiral, or that those have done who published his *Four Navigations,* in attributing the discovery of this continent to himself, without mentioning anyone but himself. Owing to this, all the foreigners who write of these Indies in Latin, or in their own mother-tongue, or who make charts or maps, call the continent America, as having been first discovered by Americo.

For as Americo was a Latinist, and eloquent, he knew how to make use of the first voyage he undertook, and to give the credit to himself, as if he had been the principal captain of it. He was only one of those who were with the captain, Alonso de Hojeda, either as a mariner, or because, as a trader, he had contributed towards the expenses of the expedition; but he secured notoriety by dedicating his *Navigations* to King René of Naples.[4] Certainly these *Navigations* unjustly usurp from the Admiral the honour and privilege of having been the first who, by his labours, industry, and the sweat of his brow, gave to Spain and to the world a knowledge of this continent, as well as of all the Western Indies. Divine Providence reserved this honour and privilege for the Admiral Don Cristóbal Colón, and for no other. For this reason no one can presume to usurp the credit, nor to give it to himself or to another, without wrong, injustice, and injury committed against the Admiral, and consequently without offence against God.

In order that this truth may be made manifest, I will here relate truthfully, and impartially, the information on the subject which I possess. To understand the matter it is necessary to bear in mind that the Admiral left San Lucar, on his third voyage, on the 30th of May 1498, and arrived at the Cape Verde Islands on the 27th of June. He sighted the island of Trinidad on Tuesday, the 31st of July, and soon afterwards, on Wednesday, the 1st of August, he saw the continent to the south of a strait two leagues wide, between it and the island of Trinidad. He called this strait the "mouth of the Serpent", and the mainland, believing it to be an island, he named Isla Sancta. Presently, on the following Friday, he sighted and discovered Paria, which he called Isla de Gracia, thinking that it also was an island. An account of all these discoveries, with a painted outline of the land, was sent by the Admiral to the Sovereigns.

This being understood, we shall now see when Americo Vespucio set out, and with whom, to discover and trade in those parts. Those who may read this history must know that, at that time, Alonso de Hojeda was in Castille, when the account of the discovery and of the form of that land arrived, which was sent by the Admiral to the Sovereigns. This report and map came into the hands of the Bishop Don Juan Rodriguez de Fonseca, afterwards Bishop of Palencia, who had charge of all business connected with the Indies from the beginning, and was then Archdeacon of Seville. The said Alonso de Hojeda was a great favourite of the Bishop, and when the report of the Admiral and the map arrived, Fonseca suggested to Hojeda to go and make more discoveries in the same direction as the Admiral had taken. For when the thread is discovered and placed in the hand, it is an easy matter to reach the skein. Hojeda was aided by the information which the Admiral had collected from the Indians when he served in the first voyage, that there was a continent behind the lands and islands then reached. As he had the favour and goodwill of the Bishop, he looked out for persons who would fit out some ships, for he himself had not sufficient funds. As he was known in Seville as a brave and distinguished man, he found, either there, or perhaps at the port of Santa Maria, whence he sailed, some one who enabled him to fit out four ships. The Sovereigns gave him his commission and instructions, and appointed him captain, for the discovery and purchase of gold and pearls, a fifth being reserved as the royal share, and to treat of peace and friendship with people he should meet with during the expedition.

Thus the first who went to discover after the Admiral was no other than Alonso de Hojeda. Those whom he took, and wanted to take in his company, consisted of the sailors who were acquainted with the voyage to those lands, who were none others but those who had come and gone with the Admiral. Those were the principal mariners of the time. One of them was Juan de la Cosa Biscayan,[5] who went with the Admiral when he discovered this island, and was afterwards with him in the Cuba and Jamaica discovery, the most laborious voyage up to that time. Hojeda also took with him the pilot Bartolomé Roldán, who was well known in this city of San Domingo, and who built, from their foundations, a great number of the houses now standing in the four streets. He too had been with the Admiral in his first voyage, and also in the discovery of Paria and the mainland. Hojeda also took the said Americo, and I do not know whether as pilot, or as a man instructed in navigation and learned in cosmography. For it appears that Hojeda puts him among the pilots he took with him.

I gather from the prologue he addressed to King René of Naples, in the book of his four *Navigations,* that the said Americo was a merchant, for so he confesses. Probably he contributed some money towards the expenses of fitting-out the four ships, with the condition of receiving a proportionate share of the profits. Although Americo asserts that the King of Castille sent out the expedition, and that they went to discover by his order, this is not true. Three or four, or ten, persons combined, who were possessed of some money, and begged and even importuned the Sovereigns for permission to go and discover and search, with the object of promoting their own profits and interests. Thus Hojeda, owing to his having got possession of the chart which the Admiral had sent home of the mainland he had discovered, for the Sovereigns, and owing to his having with him the pilots and mariners who had been with the Admiral, came to discover the further part of the mainland, which will be described in chapter 166.

It is a thing well known, and established by many witnesses, that Americo went with Alonso de Hojeda, and that Hojeda went after the Admiral had discovered the mainland. It is also proved by Alonso de Hojeda himself. He was produced as a witness in favour of the Crown, when the Admiral Don Diego Colón, next and legitimate successor of the Admiral Don Cristóbal Colón, had a lawsuit with the Crown for all the estate of which his father had been dispossessed, as he was by the same cause. Alonso de Hojeda testifies as follows, in his reply to the second question. He was asked "if he knew that the Admiral Don Cristóbal Colón had not discovered any part of what is now called mainland, except when he once touched at the part called Paria?" The answer of Hojeda was that the Admiral touched at the island of Trinidad, and passed between that island and the "Boca del Drago", which is Paria, and that he sighted the island of Margarita. Being asked how he knew this, he answered that he knew it because he, the witness, saw the chart which the said Admiral sent to Castille, to the King and Queen our Lords, of what he had discovered at that time: and also because he, the witness, soon afterwards went on his voyage of discovery, and found that the Admiral's account of what he had discovered was the truth. To the fifth question, which refers to what the same Hojeda discovered himself beyond Paria, he replied as follows: "I was the first to go on an exploring expedition after the discovery of the Admiral, and I went first nearly 200 leagues to the south on the mainland, and afterwards came to Paria, going out by the 'Boca del Drago'. There I ascertained that the Admiral had been at the island of Trinidad, bordering on the 'Boca del Drago'." Further on he says: "In the voyage which this witness undertook, he took with him Juan de la Cosa and Americo Vespucio, and other pilots."[6] Alonso de Hojeda says this, among other things, in his deposition and statement.

Two things are thus proved by Hojeda himself. One is that he took Americo with him, and the other that he undertook his voyage to the mainland, after it had been discovered by the Admiral. The latter fact is established beyond any doubt, namely, that the Admiral was the first who discovered Paria, and that he was there before any other Christian whatever was either there or on any other part of the mainland, nor had any tidings of it. The Admiral Don Diego, his son, had proof of this from sixty hearsay witnesses and twenty-five eye-witnesses, as is seen by the records of the lawsuit, which I have not only seen but thoroughly examined. It was also proved that it was owing to the Admiral having first discovered these islands of the Indies, and afterwards Paria, which is the mainland, before anyone else whatever, that the others had the courage to follow his example and become discoverers. It may be held for certain that no one would have undertaken to go on voyages of discovery, and that neither the Indies nor any part of them would have been made known if the Admiral had not led the way. This is proved by sixteen hearesay witnesses, by forty-one who believed it, by twenty who knew it, and by thirteen who gave evidence that in their belief the Admiral made his discoveries before anyone else whatever. Peter Martyr also gives the same testimony in his first Decade, chapters 8 and 9. This author deserves more credit than any of those who have written in Latin, because he was in Castille at the time, and knew all the explorers, and they were glad to tell him all they had seen and discovered, as a man in authority; and because he made his inquiries with a view to writing, as we mentioned in the prologue of the history.

Americo confesses in his first *Navigation* that he arrived at Paria during his first voyage, saying: "*Et provincia ipsa Parias ab ipsis nuncupata est.*" Afterwards he made the second *Navigation*, also with Hojeda, as will appear in chapter 162.

Here it is important to note and make clear the error made by the world in general respecting America. What I say is this: As no one had arrived at nor seen Paria before the Admiral, and as the next explorer who arrived was Hojeda, it follows that either Americo was with Hojeda, or came after him. If he was with Hojeda, Hojeda was after the Admiral. The Admiral left San Lucar on the 30th of May, and came in sight of Trinidad and the mainland on the last day of July, and the 1st and 3rd of August, as has been proved. How, therefore, can Americo say, without a perversion of the truth, that he left Cadiz in his first *Navigation* on the 20th of May of the year of our salvation 1497? The falsehood is clear, and if the statement was made by him in earnest, he committed a great infamy. Even if it is not an intentional falsehood, it seems to be so; for he gives himself an advantage of ten days as regards the Admiral, with reference to the departure from Cadiz, for the Admiral left San Lucar on the 30th of May, and Americo alleges that he departed from Cadiz on the 20th of that month, and also usurps a year, for the Admiral sailed in 1498, while Americo pretends that he set out on his first *Navigation* in the year 1497. It is true that there would seem to be a mistake, and not an intentional fraud in this, for Americo says that his first *Navigation* occupied eighteen months, and at the end he asserts that the date of his return to Cadiz was the 15th of October 1499. If he left Cadiz on the 20th of May 1497, the voyage occupied twenty-nine months: seven in the year 1497, all the year 1498, and ten months in the year 1499. It is possible that 1499 may be a misprint for 1498[7] in treating of the return to Castille, and if this was so, there can be no doubt that the fraud was intentional. This fraud or mistake, whichever it may have been, and the power of writing and narrating well and in good style, as well as Americo's silence respecting the name of his captain, which was Hojeda, and his care to mention no one but himself, and his dedication to King René, these things have led foreign writers to name our mainland AMERICA, as if Americo alone, and not another with him, had made the discovery before all others. It is manifest what injustice he did if he intentionally usurped what belonged to another, namely, to the Admiral Don Cristóbal Colón, and with what good reason this discovery, and all its consequences, should belong to the Admiral, after the goodness and providence of God, which chose him for this work. As it belongs more to him, the said continent ought to be called Columba, after Colón, or Columbo, who discovered it, or else "Sancta" or "De Gracia", the names he himself gave it, and not America after Americo.

CHAPTER CLXIV

The Admiral sent five ships[8] with the news of the discovery of the mainland of Paria, and of the pearls. Alonşo de Hojeda was then in Spain. I believe myself that he returned at the same time as my uncle, Francisco de Penalosa, knowing that the Admiral had discovered that land and the pearls, and having seen the chart of the new discoveries which the Admiral had sent to the Sovereigns, and that the Admiral said in his letters that it was an island, although he was also inclined to the belief that it was a continent; and being favoured by the Bishop of Badajos, Don Juan de Fonseca, who superintended and managed everything, Hojeda petitioned that he might have license to discover in those parts either continent, or islands, or whatever he might find. The Bishop gave the licence, signed with his own signature, and not with that of the Sovereign, either because the Sovereigns ordered him to grant such licenses, or this one only, which is hard to believe; or because he wished to make the grant of his own authority, and without giving the Sovereigns a share in the matter, the Admiral having complained to the Sovereigns in the year 1495 that it was in opposition to his privileges to give a licence to anyone to undertake discoveries. . . . I do not see how the Bishop was able to grant the licence in the way he did. But I quite see that as he was a very determined and obstinate man, and was hostile to the Admiral's interests, he may have taken this step actuated by his own audacity, and without consulting the Sovereigns. This is possible, but still I doubt it; for, although he was very intimate with the Sovereigns, this was hardly a thing that he would have dared to do on his own authority. The licence was granted with the limitations that it did not include the territory of the King of Portugal, nor the lands discovered by the Admiral up to the year 1495. Another question arises here: Why was not the land excepted which the Admiral had just discovered, and which was identified by the letters and the chart he had sent to the Sovereigns? To this I cannot give an answer.

That the licence was only signed by the said Bishop, and not by the Sovereigns, there can be no doubt, for Francisco Roldán saw it, and so described it to the Admiral, and I saw Roldán's original letter, as I will presently mention.

Hojeda having obtained the licence, he found persons in Seville who would fit out four caravels or ships, for there were many who were eager to go and discover by means of the thread which the Admiral had put into their hands. For he was the first who opened the gates of that Ocean Sea, which had been closed for so many ages.

Hojeda set out from the port of Santa Maria or of Cadiz in the month of May. If Americo Vespucio does not speak contrary to the truth as regards the day of the month, he does so as regards the year. The date of Hojeda's departure was the 20th of May 1499, not 1497, as Americo says, usurping the honour and glory which belongs to the Admiral, and assuming the whole for himself alone, wishing to give the world to understand that he was the first discoverer of the mainland of Paria, and not the Admiral, to whom is justly and rightfully due all the discovery of all these islands and mainland of the Indies, as has already been proved in chapter 140. In that chapter I endeavoured to leave it doubtful whether Americo had, with intention, tacitly denied that this discovery was made first by the Admiral, and had given the credit of it to himself alone. For I had not then seen what I afterwards gathered from those writings of Americo, and from other writings of those times in my possession, or which I have found. From these I conclude that it was a most false and dishonest thing on the part of Americo to wish to usurp against justice the honour due to the Admiral. The proof of this falsehood is made clear from the evidence of Americo himself, in this way. We will assume what has already been proved in chapter 140, namely:—First, the testimony of such a multitude of witnesses who knew that the Admiral was the first who discovered the mainland of Paria, and consequently no one reached any part of the mainland before him, this being also affirmed by Peter Martyr in the third and ninth chapters of his first Decade; and Hojeda himself, in his deposition, also testified, being unable to deny it, saying that after he had seen the chart in Castille he went to discover, and found that the Admiral had previously arrived at Paria and gone out by the Boca del Drago. Secondly, Americo went with Hojeda, either as a pilot or as one who knew something of the sea, for he is mentioned jointly with Juan de la Cosa and other pilots; or perhaps he went as an adventurer, contributing part of the expenses and having a share in the profits. Thirdly, we refer to what Americo confesses in his first *Navigation*, which is, that he reached a place called Paria by the Indian natives; also, that in a certain part or province of the coast of the mainland, or in an island where they made war, the Indians wounded twenty-two men and killed one. Now this happened in 1499, as I shall presently prove. What we say is this: The Admiral was the first who discovered the mainland and Paria, Hojeda was the first after the Admiral, and Americo, who went with Hojeda, confesses that they arrived at Paria. The Admiral left San Lucar on the 30th of May 1498; presently, Hojeda and Americo left Cadiz in the following year, 1499. If the Admiral left San Lucar on the 30th of May, and Hojeda and Americo sailed from Cadiz on the 20th of May, and the Admiral departed first, it is clear that the departure of Hojeda and Americo could not have been in that year of 1498, but in the following year of 1499. Even if it can be said that Hojeda and Americo may have departed first on the 20th of May of the same year of 1498 that the Admiral sailed, still the statement of Americo would be false, for he said that he departed in 1497. Now there is no doubt that Hojeda and Americo neither departed in 1497 nor in 1498, but in 1499, and it is, therefore, demonstrated that it was not Americo who first discovered the mainland of Paria, nor anyone else but the Admiral. This is confirmed by what was shown in chapter 140, that Hojeda, in his deposition when he was called as a witness before the Fiscal, said that after he had seen the chart of the land discovered by the Admiral, when he was in Castille, he went on a voyage of discovery himself, and found that the land was as it had been correctly laid down on the chart. Now the Admiral sent this chart with a report to the Sovereigns in the year 1498; on the 18th of October the said ships left Navidad, and my father was on board one of them. Afterwards Hojeda and Americo sailed on the 20th of May, as Americo himself writes, and this can only have been in the following year, 1499. This is confirmed by another reason. The Admiral was informed by the Christians who were in the province of Yaquimo that Hojeda had arrived at the land called

Brasil on the 5th of September, and the Admiral wrote to this effect to the Sovereigns by the ships in which the Procurators of the Admiral and of Roldán went home. This was in the year 1499, at the time when Francisco Roldán and his company were about to be, or had been, induced to yield obedience to the Admiral. This was the first voyage that Americo made with Hojeda. It is, therefore, clear that neither Hojeda nor Americo can have left Cadiz in 1497, but they must have sailed in 1499. That this was the first voyage made by Hojeda and Americo in search of the mainland appears from two reasons which have already been mentioned as being given by Americo himself in his first *Navigation*. One is, that they arrived at a land called by the natives Paria, and the other that the Indians wounded twenty-two men and killed one in a certain island. This latter fact was told to Francisco Roldán by Hojeda's people when the same Roldán went on board the ships of Hojeda. The Admiral sent him as soon as he was informed that Hojeda had reached the land of Brasil.[9]

Francisco Roldán wrote to the Admiral from thence these, among other words which I saw in the handwriting of Francisco Roldán, his handwriting being well known to me. The letter begins as follows:—"I make known to your Lordship that I arrived where Hojeda was on Sunday the 29th of September," etc., and he goes on: "this being so, my Lord, I went on board the caravels, and found in them Juan Velasquez and Juan Vizcaíno,[10] who showed me a concession made to him for the discovery of new countries, signed by the Lord Bishop, by which he was granted permission to make discoveries in these parts so long as he did not touch the territory of the King of Portugal, nor the territory which had been discovered by your Lordship up to the year 1495. They made discoveries in the land which your Lordship recently discovered. He says that they sailed along the coast for 600 leagues, where they encountered people who fought with them, wounding twenty and killing one. In some places they landed and were received with great honour, and in others the natives would not consent to their landing."

These are the words of Francisco Roldán to the Admiral. Americo, in his first *Navigation*, says:—"But one of our people was killed and twenty-two wounded, all recovering their health by the help of God." The same Americo also relates that Hojeda and himself arrived at the island Española, as will appear presently. It appears clearly from the evidence of the said Americo, and the agreement of his statement with what his companions told to Francisco Roldán, that they had twenty or twenty-two wounded and one killed, and this was during his first voyage. It also appears from both that they went to and saw Paria, and the coast newly discovered by the Admiral. If this was the first voyage of Americo, and he came to this island in the year 1499, on the 5th of September, having left Cadiz on the 20th of May of the same year, 1499, as has been distinctly shown, it follows that Americo has falsely stated that he left Cadiz in the year 1497. This is also shown by what the Admiral wrote to the Sovereigns when he knew that Hojeda had sailed five months before, in May. He wrote as follows:—"Hojeda arrived at the port where the brasil is, five days ago. These sailors say that as the time is so short since his departure from Castille, he cannot have discovered land, but he may well have got a lading of brasil before it could be prohibited, and as he has done, so may other interlopers." These are the words of the Admiral, and I have seen them in his own handwriting. He intended to explain that little land could have been discovered in five months, and that, if he had not sent Francisco Roldán to prohibit the ships from taking a cargo of brasil, they might easily have done so and have departed, and that the same might be done by any other stranger, unless steps were taken to prevent it.

All these proofs, taken from the letters of the Admiral and of Roldán, cannot be disputed, because they are most certainly authentic, and no doubt can be thrown on any of them. For no one then could tell that this matter would be alleged and brought forward, seeing that during fifty-six or fifty-seven years what was written told a different story, which was the truth, nor was there anything to conceal.

But what Americo has written to make himself famous and give himself credit, tacitly usurping the discovery of the continent which belongs to the Admiral, was done with intention. This is shown by many arguments given in this chapter and in chapter 140. But besides these verbal proofs, I desire to submit others which make the thing most manifest. One is that he inverted the voyages he made, applying the first to the second, and making out that things which belonged to one happened in the other. He asserts that in the first voyage they were absent eighteen months, and this is not possible, for after being absent from Castille for five months they came to this island, and they could not have returned again to the mainland to coast along it for such a distance, owing to contrary winds and currents, except with great difficulty and after a long time. Thus his voyage to the continent only took five months, within which time he arrived here, as has been already explained, and as Hojeda told some of the Spaniards who were here, before he left his island. He then made an inroad on some of the surrounding islands, seizing some of the natives and carrying them off to Castille. According to the statement of Americo, they took 222 slaves, and this occurs at the end of his first *Navigation*. "And we, following the way to Spain, at length arrived at the port of Cadiz with 222 captured persons," etc.

Another statement is that certain injuries and violences done by Hojeda and his followers against the Indians and Spaniards in Xaragua in his first voyage is placed by Americo at the end of his second *Navigation*. He there says: "We departed, and, for the sake of obtaining many things of which we were in need, we shaped a course for the island of Antiglia, being that which Christopher Columbus discovered a few years ago. Here we took many supplies on board, and remained two months and seventeen days. Here we endured many dangers and troubles from the same Christians who were in this island with Columbus. I believe this was caused by envy, but, to avoid prolixity, I will refrain from recounting what happened." The Portuguese then called this island of Española Antilla, and this Americo used the word Antiglia, because he was writing in Lisbon. In the following chapter I will explain what these troubles from the Spaniards were, and what caused them, which he excuses himself from dwelling upon in order to avoid prolixity. It will then be clearly seen that they happened during his first voyage.

Another point is that they arrived at this island on the 5th of September, as he said, and that they remained, according to him, for two months and two days—that is, all of September and October, and two more days of November. He there says that they left this island on the 22nd of July and arrived at the port of Cadiz on the 8th of September. All this is most false. The same may be said of the dates of all the years, months, and days which Americo gives in his *Navigations*. It thus appears that he designedly wished to take the glory and renown of the discovery of the continent, even keeping silence respecting the name of his own captain, Alonso de Hojeda, and tacitly usurping, as has been said, the honour and glory which belongs to the Admiral for this famous deed, deceiving the world by writing in Latin, and to the

King René of Naples, there being no one to resist or expose his claim out of Spain, those who then knew the truth being kept in ignorance. I am surprised that Don Hernando Colón, son of the same Admiral, and a person of good judgment and ability, and having in his possession these same *Navigations* of Americo, as I know, did not take notice of this injury and usurpation which Americo Vespucio did to his most illustrious father.

CHAPTER CLXV

There remains the demonstrations, now proved in detail, of the industrious contrivance of Americo Vespucio, not at first easily conceived, as I believe, but thought out at some subsequent time, by which he attributed to himself the discovery of the greater part of that Indian world, when God had conceded that privilege to the Admiral. Now it is proper to continue the history of what happened to Alonso de Hojeda, with whom Americo went on his first voyage. He departed from the port of Cadiz with four ships, in the month of May. Juan de la Cosa, with all the experience acquired in his voyages with the Admiral, went as pilot, and there were other pilots and persons who had served in the said voyages. Americo also embarked, as has already been mentioned in chapter 140, either as a merchant, or as one versed in cosmography and studies relating to the sea. They sailed in May, according to Americo, but not, as he says, in the year 1497, the true date being 1499, as has already been sufficiently proved. Their course was directed towards the west, to the Canary Islands, then southward. After twenty-seven days[11] (according to the said Americo) they came in sight of land, which they believed to be continental, and they were not deceived. Having come to the nearest land, they anchored at a distance of about a league from the shore, from fear of striking on some sunken rock. They got out the boats, put arms into them, and reached the beach, where they saw an immense number of naked people. They received them with great joy. But the Indians looked on with astonishment, and presently ran away to the nearest forest. The Christians approached them with signs of peace and friendship, but they would not trust the strangers. As the Christians had anchored in an open roadstead, and not in a port, wishing to be out of danger if bad weather came on, they weighed, and stood along the coast to seek for a port, all the shore being crowded with people. After two days they found a good port. *(Las Casas then quotes the account of the natives given by Americo Vespucci, respecting which he makes the following comments.)* Americo relates all these things in his first *Navigation,* many of which he could not have known in two, nor three, nor in ten days that he may have been among the Indians, not knowing a single word of their language, as he himself confesses. Such are the statements, that owing to the heat of the sun they move from place to place every eight years; that when the women are enraged with their husbands they create abortions; that they have no rule or order in their marriages; that they have neither king nor lord nor chief in their wars; and others of the same kind. Therefore we can only believe those statements which are based on what he actually saw or might see, such as what the natives ate and drank, that they went naked, that they were of such and such colour, were great swimmers, and other external acts. The rest appears to be all fiction.

CHAPTER CLXVI

They left these people and proceeded along the coast, often landing and having intercourse with different tribes, until they arrived at a port where, as they entered, they saw a town built over the water like Venice. Americo says that it contained twenty very large houses, built, like the others he had seen, in the shape of a bell, and raised on very strong piles. At the doors of the houses they had drawbridges, by which, as if they were streets, they went from one house to another. *(Las Casas then gives the account of the encounter with the natives of this town on piles, just as it is given by Vespucci.)* They made sail from this port, and proceeded for eighty leagues along the coast; and this was the land of Paria discovered by the Admiral, as has already been shown. Here they found another people, with very different customs and language. They anchored and got into their boats to go on shore, where they found over 4,000 natives on the beach. The Indians were so frightened that they did not wait, but fled to the mountains. The Christians having landed, followed a path, and came to many huts, which they believed were those of fishermen. Here they found fish of various kinds, and also one of the *iguanas* which I have already described, and which astonished them, for they thought it was some very fierce serpent. The bread eaten by these people, says Americo, was made with fish steeped in hot water, and afterwards pounded. From this mass small loaves were kneaded and baked, making very good bread, in his judgment. They found many kinds of fruits and herbs; but they not only took nothing, but left many small things from Castille in the huts, in the hope that thus the fears of the natives would be dispelled, and the Spaniards then returned to the ships. *(Las Casas here inserts the account given by Vespucci of a journey inland, and of intercourse with these natives.)* Americo then says that the land was populous, and also full of many different animals, few being like those of Spain. He mentions lions, bears, deer, pigs, wild goats, which had a certain deformity, and were unlike ours. But in truth

I do not believe that he saw either lions or bears, because lions are very rare, and there cannot have been so many as that he should see them; and the same remark applies to bears. No one who has been to the Indies has even seen goats there, nor can I understand how he can have seen the difference between deer and goats nor how he can have seen pigs, there being none in those parts. Deer he may well have seen, as there are many on the mainland. He says there are no horses, mules, asses, cows, nor sheep, nor dogs, and here he tells the truth, although there is a kind of dog in some parts. He says that there is great abundance of other wild animals of various kinds, but if they were not rabbits he could have little true evidence of having seen them. Of birds of different plumage and species he says that he saw many; and this I believe, for there is an infinite number. He says that the region is pleasant and fertile, full of woods and great forests, which consist of evergreens, yielding fruits of many sorts; and all this is also true.

He then repeats that many people came to see the whiteness and persons of the Spaniards. (I do not know whether he is speaking of this same land, as it would seem, or of another, for he appears to confuse his account here with what he had said before, that they had to depart that night.) He tells us that the natives asked whence the Spaniards came, and they replied that they had come down from heaven to see the things of the earth, which the Indians undoubtedly believed. Here the Christians committed a great sacrilege, thinking to make an agreeable offering to God. As they saw the natives so gentle, meek, and tractable, although neither could understand a single word of what the other said, and therefore the Spaniards could not teach the Indians any doctrine, yet, says Americo, they baptized an infinite number; whence it appears how little Americo, and those who were with him, appreciated the practice of the sacraments and the reverence that is due to them, nor even the disposition and frame of mind with which they should be received. It is manifest that those Christians, in baptizing the natives, committed a great offence against God. Americo says that after they were baptized, the Indians used the world *charaybi*, which means that they called the Spaniards men of great knowledge. This statement is a thing to laugh at, for the Spaniards did not even know the Indian names for bread or for water, which are among the first that we learn in acquiring a language; yet during the few days they remained Americo wants us to believe that he understood that *charaybi* signifies men of great knowledge. Here Americo declares that the natives called this land *Paria*; and he conceals, what he must have known, that the Admiral had already been there several days, which was a reason for not remaining silent.

CHAPTER CLXVII

They decided upon leaving this port and the sweet-water gulf formed by the island of Trinidad and the mainland of Paria by the "Boca del Drago", and I suspect that, as this was a place which was notoriously discovered by the Admiral, Americo kept silence as to the name of "Boca del Drago" intentionally. For it is certain that Hojeda and Americo were within this port, because the same Hojeda gave evidence to that effect on oath, as well as many other witnesses also on oath, as is affirmed in the evidence taken by the Fiscal. Here Americo says that the voyage had now lasted thirteen months, but I do not believe it. Even if he tells the truth as regards the number of months, this must have been in the second voyage, which he afterwards made with the same Hojeda, as I think must be understood, and not in this first voyage, as is shown, for many reasons already set forth, and for others which will hereafter be given. Finally departing from Paria, they proceeded along the coast and arrived at Margarita, an island sighted by the Admiral and named by him Margarita, although he did not stop there. Hojeda landed and walked over part of it, as he himself says, and those same witnesses who were with them also say that he arrived there, though they neither deny nor affirm that he landed; but there need be no doubt of it, for it is a pleasant island. This, however, little affects the question. It may be believed that they here bartered for pearls, although he does not say so, for other discoverers who came after him traded at the island of Margarita. Hojeda extended his journey to the providence and gulf called Cuquibacoa in the language of the Indians, which is now named Venezuela in our language, and thence to Cabo de la Vela, where they now fish for pearls. He gave it that name of Cabo de la Vela, which it still retains; and a row of islands running east and west was discovered, some of which were called the Islands of the Giants.

Thus had Hojeda coasted the mainland for 400 leagues, 200 to the east of Paria, where he sighted the first land, and this was the only land that he and those with him discovered. Paria and Margarita were discovered by the Admiral, as well as a great part of the said 200 leagues from Margarita to Cabo de la Vela, for the Admiral saw the chain of mountains to the westward as he sailed along, so that all this discovery is due to him. For it does not follow that, in order to be the discoverer of a land or island, a navigator must have passed along the whole of it. For instance, it is clear that the island of Cuba was personally discovered by the Admiral, and for this it is not necessary that he should have gone into every corner of it; and the same remark applies to Española and the other islands, and also the mainland, however large it may be, and however far it may extend, the Admiral discovered it.

From this it appears that Americo exaggerated when he said that in his first *Navigation* they sailed along the coast for 860 leagues. This is not true, as is proved by the confession of Hojeda, a man who had no desire to lose anything of his own glory and rights, for he said, as appeared in chapter 140, that he discovered 200 leagues beyond Paria, and the coast from Paria to Cuquibacoa, which is now Venezuela. I have added as far as Cabo de la Vela, because I found it so deposed in the process by several witnesses who afterwards knew all that land well, had intercourse with the discoverers, and went with them in their voyages of discovery, though not in that voyage of Hojeda; but the testimony was given when the events were recent, and consequently well known. Hojeda himself did not mention Cabo de la Vela, because it is near the Gulf of Venezuela, and is all one land; and of the gulf and province he made principal mention, as a thing notable and important, and called by the natives Cuquibacoa.

Along all this land or sea-coast traversed by Hojeda, Americo, and his company, they got gold and pearls by barter and exchange, but the quantity is not known, nor the deeds they perpetrated in the land. Having left Margarita, they went to Cumaná and Maracapana, which are respectively seven and twenty leagues from Margarita. There are people on the sea-shore, and before reaching Cumaná there is a gulf where the water of the sea forms a great angle extending fourteen leagues into the land, round which there are numerous and populous tribes. The first, nearly at the mouth of the bay, is Cumaná. A large river falls into the sea near the village, in which there are numbers of the creatures we call *lagartos*, but they are nothing more than the crocodiles of the river Nile. As they were under the necessity of refitting the ships, they being defective for so long a voyage as a return to Spain, and also being in want of provisions, they arrived at a port which

Americo calls the best in the world. But he does not say where it was, nor does he mention Hojeda. According to what I remember forty-three years after having been there, and over fifty years since the voyage of Hojeda, I suspect that it must be a gulf called Cariaco, which runs fourteen leagues into the land, the entrance being seven leagues from Margarita, on the mainland near Cumaná. Further, it occurs to me that I heard that at that time Hojeda entered and repaired his ships, and built a brigantine in the port called Maracapana, but this, though a port, is not the best in the world.

At last they left the port, wherever it may have been, within those 200 leagues of mainland from Paria onwards. They were received and served by the people of that region, who were innumerable, according to Americo, as if they had been angels from heaven, and as Abraham had known the three, so they were recognised as angels. They unloaded the ships and brought them to land, always helped by the labour of the Indians. They careened and cleared them, and built a new brigantine. They say that during all the time that they were there, which was thirty-seven days, they never had any need of touching their Castilian provisions, because they were supplied with deer, fish, native bread, and other food; and if they had not been so provided, says Americo, they would have been in great distress for provisions in returning to Spain. During all the time they were there they went on shore among the villages, in which they were received with hospitality, honour, and festivity. This is certain (as will be seen further on in the course of the history, if it please the all-powerful God), that all these people of the Indies, being by nature most simple and kind, know well how to serve and please those who come to them, when they look upon them as friends. When after having repaired their ships and built the brigantine they determined to return to Spain, Americo here says that their hosts made great complaints of another cruel and ferocious tribe, inhabiting an island at a distance of 100 leagues; saying that they came at a certain time of the year over the sea, to make war, and that they carried off their captives, killing and eating them. They showed their grief with so much feeling and persistency, says Americo, that it moved us to compassion, and we offered to avenge them. This made them rejoice greatly, says Americo, and they said they would like to go also. But the Christians, for many reasons, would only consent that seven natives should accompany them, on condition that they should not be taken back to their country in the ships, but that they should return in their own canoes, and to this, he says, both parties consented. I do not know what interpreter made these agreements, nor who understood all that was said, but it is obvious that they could not have known the language in thirty-seven days. And how could Hojeda and Americo, and those of their company, know whether the islanders had just cause for war or not? Were these men so certain of the justice of the natives that, without further delay, merely because they made complaints, they offered to avenge them? Pray God that they did not make this war to fill up their ships with natives, with a view to selling them for slaves, as they afterwards did in Cadiz; work too often done by our people against these unfortunate tribes and lands. They set out, and after seven days they came upon numerous islands, some peopled and others uninhabited, says Americo, at last arriving at their destination. These islands cannot be others than those we reach in coming from Spain, such as Dominica and Guadalupe, and the others that lie in that line. Presently they saw, he says, a great crowd of people, who, when they saw the ships and the boats approaching the shore well armed with guns, sent a body of 400 to the water's edge, with many women, naked and armed with bows and arrows and shields, and all painted in different colours, and adorned with wings and feathers of large birds, so that they appeared very warlike and fierce. When the boats had approached to the distance of a cross-bow shot, they advanced into the water, and discharged a great number of arrows to prevent their advance. The Christians discharged the firearms and killed many of them, and fearing the discharge and the firing, they left the water and came on shore. A body of forty-two men then landed from the boats and attacked them. The natives did not fly, but stood their ground manfully, and fought valiantly like lions, defending themselves and their country. They fought for two long hours, first with their guns and cross-bows, and afterwards with their swords and lances, killing many; and that they might not all perish, those of the natives who were able, fled into the woods. Thus the Christians remained victorious, and they returned to their ships with great joy at having sent so many people to hell who had never offended them. On another day, in the morning, they saw a great multitude of natives, making the air resound with horns and trumpets, painted and armed for a second battle.

The Christians determined to send fifty-seven men against them, divided into four companies, each with a captain, intending, says Americo, to make friends with them if possible, but if not, to treat them as enemies, and to make slaves of as many as they could take. This is said by Americo, and it is to be noted here how he makes a pretext of truth and justice and legality, when the Spaniards had promised to go a hundred leagues on a message of war and vengeance. Yet they would come to treat of friendship with the natives, seeking occasion to gratify their covetousness, which was what they came for from Castille. Such are the pretexts and unworthy artifices that have always been used for the destruction of these natives.

They went on shore, but the Indians, owing to the fire from the guns, did not venture to oppose their landing, yet they awaited them with great steadiness. The naked men fought against the clothed men with great valour for a long time, but the clothed made a fearful slaughter among the naked men, the swords taking great effect on their naked bodies. The survivors fled when they saw that they were being cut to pieces. The Christians pursued them to a village, capturing all they could, to the number of twenty-five. They returned with their victory, but with the loss of one killed and twenty-two wounded. They then sent away the seven natives who had come with them from the mainland. They departed, says Americo, taking with them as prisoners seven natives given to them by the Spaniards, three men and four women, as their captives, and they were very joyful, admiring that deed performed by the forces of the Christians. All this is related by Americo, who adds that they returned to Spain and arrived at Cadiz with 222 Indian captives, where they were, according to him, very joyfully received, and where they sold all the slaves. Who will now ask whence they stole and carried off the 200 natives? This, as other things, is passed over in silence by Americo. It should be noted here by readers who know something of what belongs to right and natural justice, that although these natives are without faith, yet those with whom Americo went had neither just cause nor right to make war on the natives of those islands and to carry them off as slaves, without having received any injury from them, nor the slightest offence. Moreover, they were ignorant whether the accusations of those of the mainland against the islanders were just or unjust. What report, or what love would be spread about and sown among the natives, touching those Christians, when they left them wounded and desolate? But we must proceed, for, touching this matter, *grandis restat nobis via.*

CHAPTER CLXVIII

Here Americo is convicted of a palpable falsehood, for he says that he went to Castille from that island where he perpetrated such atrocities, making no mention of having first gone to Española, as he did. He refers the visit to Española to his second voyage, but this is not true, as has already been proved in chapter 162. It is not the fact that they went to Castille from the Island where they made war and ill-treated the people: as can be proved from the witnesses examined before the Royal Fiscal, in the lawsuit between Don Diego Colón and the King respecting the granting and observance of his privileges, of which I have often made mention before. They deposed that Alonso de Hojeda, with whom Americo sailed in his first voyage, when along the coast to Cuquibacoa, which is Venezuela, and the Cabo de la Vela, and that thence they went to Española. Thus a witness named Andres de Morales made oath, whom I knew well, a principal pilot and a veteran of these Indies, citizen of Santo Domingo. He said in his deposition, in answer to the fifth question, as follows: "that he knew what happened during that voyage." Asked how he knew, he said: "that he knew because he had often been with Juan de la Cosa and with Alonso de Hojeda, and talked over this voyage, and that they went from the island of Roquemes in the Canaries, and arrived at the mainland near the province of Paria, passing on to the island of Margarita, thence to Maracapana, discovering the coast as far as the Cacique Ayarayte, and thence, from port to port, to the Island of the Giants, the province of Cuquibacoa, and the Cabo de la Vela, which name was given to it by the said Hojeda and Juan de la Cosa, and thence they went to the island of Española." These are his words. Now they could not go from a place so far to leeward, to the island where they committed their depredations, because it must have been one of those towards the east, such as Guadalupe, and the islands near it. It would be very difficult to work to windward against wind and current, which are continuous. This is confirmed by the fact that they reached Brasil in Española, which is the port of Yaquimo,[12] and the proper and natural landfall from Cabo de la Vela. If they had repaired the ships and taken in provisions in that port of the mainland, how was it that it was found necessary to repair and take in provisions again at Española? How was it that the witnesses, and especially the pilot, Andres de Morales, who seems to intimate that he went with them, do not mention that Hojeda had built a brigantine and repaired his ships in some port of the mainland, that being a remarkable event. It would strengthen the veracity of his statements with reference to the discovery of that mainland having been made by him, which was the object of the suit presided over by the Fiscal against the Admiral. It is clear that Americo transferred things which happened in the first voyage to the second, while events of the second are referred to the first voyage, as we have demonstrated already in chapter 142, being silent respecting many things, and adding others which never happened. For example, the building of the brigantine and repairing of the ships on the mainland certainly happened, and I know that it was so, being notorious at that time; but it was during the second voyage, and not the first; while the coming to the island Española, where certain scandals were caused by Hojeda, to which I shall presently refer, took place in the first voyage, and not in the second, as Americo represents. I further say that Hojeda never came to discover, trade, or settle on the mainland, without visiting Española. But his coming in the first voyage is denied or concealed by Americo by silence. From the time that Hojeda left Spain until he arrived at Española there was an interval of five months, which does not leave time for all that he is said to have done during that first voyage.

Returning to the first voyage of Hojeda, with whom Americo went by the correct route, and not by the interpolated and confused way alleged by Americo, we say that from the province of Cuquibacoa, now called Venezuela, and the Cabo de la Vela, he came to this island of Española, and anchored on the 5th of September, as I have already said in chapter 164, at Brasil, which is in the province of Yaquimo, and I even believe further down, near that which is now called Cabana, the land and dominion of a king named Haniguayabá. The Spaniards, who were in that province of Yaquimo, presently knew of the arrival, either from the Indians, or because they saw the vessels come in from the sea. They knew that it was Hojeda, and word was presently sent to the Admiral, who was at San Domingo, having recently made peace with Roldán and his companions. The Admiral ordered two or three caravels to be got ready, and sent Roldán with a force to prohibit the cutting of brasil wood, suspecting that Hojeda would load with it. Roldán was also ordered to prevent the new comer from doing any other mischief, as Hojeda was known to be most audacious in doing what he chose, it being a word and a deed with him, as they say. Roldán arrived at the port of Yaquimo, or near it, with his caravels, and landed on the 29th of that month of September. He then learnt from the Indians that Hojeda was close by. Roldán, with twenty-six of his men, came within a league and a half, and sent five men by night, as spies, to see what force was with Hojeda. They found that he was coming to reconnoitre

Roldán, for the Indians had told him that Roldán had arrived with a large force in three caravels. Roldán was known and feared in all that land, and the natives told Hojeda that Roldán had sent for him to come where he was; but this was not the case. Hojeda only had fifteen men with him, having left the rest in his four ships, which were in a port at a distance of eight leagues. He had come to get bread in the village of the cacique Haniguayabá, and they were making it, not venturing to do anything else, fearing that Roldán would come to seize them. Hojeda, with five or six men, came to where Roldán was, and entered into general conversation, Roldán inquiring how Hojeda had come to that island, and especially to that part of it, without leave from the Admiral, and why he had not first gone to where the Admiral was. Hojeda answered that he was on a voyage of discovery, and that he was in great need of provisions and his ships of repairs, so that he had no other alternative, and that he could not reach any nearer place. Roldán then asked him by what right he was making discoveries, and whether he had a royal licence that he could show to entitle him to get supplies without asking the permission of the governor. He answered that he had such a licence, but that it was on board his ship, eight leagues distant. Roldán said that it must be shown to him, otherwise he would be unable to give an account to the Admiral concerning the business on which he had been sent. Hojeda complied as far as he was able, saying that when he was despatched from that port he would go to make his reverence to the Admiral, and to tell him many things, some of which he mentioned to Roldán. These were, I have no doubt, the questions then spoken of at Court, touching the deprivation of the Admiral, for, as Roldán wrote, they were things which were not fit to be discussed in letters.

Roldán left Hojeda there and went with his caravels to the place where the caravels of Hojeda were at anchor, and found some persons on board who had been in Española with the Admiral, and had served with him in the discovery of Paria, having returned in the five ships, especially one Juan Velasquez and Juan Vizcaíno,[13] who showed him the concession signed by the Bishop Don Juan de Fonseca, which I have already mentioned in chapter 164. They informed him of the events of the voyage, and how much of the mainland they had discovered, and how they had lost one man killed, and twenty or more wounded, in a fight, as was stated in the said chapter 164, in which it is proved that this happened during the first voyage of Hojeda. Francisco Roldán also learnt from them that they had found gold, and brought it in the form of *guaninas*, which are certain trinkets, well and artificially worked, such as they know how to make in Castille, but the gold was below the standard. They brought antlers, and said they had seen deer, rabbits, and the skin of a tiger cat; also a collar made of the nails of animals, all which was news to those who lived in Española. Roldán, knowing this, and believing that Hojeda would do what he had promised; that is, that when he had got his supply of bread in that village he wold go to the port of San Domingo to visit the Admiral by land, ordered the caravels to do what they had to do, and I believe this was to get a cargo of brasil wood. Roldán went from Yaquimo to Xaragua, a distance of eighteen leagues, and visited the Christians who were allotted to the villages of the Indians, doing what seemed best to him, and then returned to report the things that had been said to him by Hojeda to the Admiral, which could not have been the best news in the world; for when the five ships came with intelligence of the rebellion of Roldán, they discussed at court the deposition of the Admiral, a thing which Hojeda would not be the last to know, being favoured by the Bishop Don Juan de Fonseca, and neither being friendly to the Admiral and his affairs. As regards the Bishop this was quite notorious, and I saw it with my eyes, felt it with my feeling, and understood it with my understanding. As to Hojeda, it appeared afterwards that he must have left Española, discontented with the Admiral.

CHAPTER CLXIX

Roldán took leave of Hojeda, believing that everything that glittered was gold, and Hojeda, having got the bread about which he had arranged, instead of taking the road to Santo Domingo to see the Admiral, and give an account to him of what he had done during his voyage, as he had promised to Roldán, and to report the news from Castille, went with his four ships towards the west, in the direction of the gulf and port of Xaragua. The Christians who were living there, in the villages of the Caciques, received him with joy, and gave him and his people all they needed, although not from the sweat of their own brows, but from that of the Indians, for of the latter the Spaniards are accustomed to be very liberal. As one of their caravels was very unseaworthy, and could no longer be kept above water, they made the Indians work, and they gave much help until she was repaired, assisting in every other way that was needed. While he was there he found that there were people who regretted the free life they had been so recently leading under Roldán, who were ill-disposed towards the affairs of the Admiral, and who were discontented because they could not now do as they pleased. One of their most common complaints was that their wages were not paid. Hojeda, moved either by the disposition he found in these people, or by the expectation of profit for himself, began to encourage the discontent, saying that he would join with them, and, uniting them with his own people, that he would go to the Admiral and demand payment in the name of the Sovereigns, and force him to pay, even if he did so unwillingly. He declared that he had powers from the Sovereigns to do this, and that he and Alonso de Carvajal had received them, when the Admiral returned in the year 1498, that they might come and constrain him to make the payments. He added many other arguments, according to what they said, in great prejudice of the Admiral, and to excite the people against him, to which the greater part inclined, being unprincipled men, friends of turbulence and unrest, and without fear either of God or of the mischief that would follow in that island, both to Christians and Indians.

There were some, however, who did not wish to join in the foolish and evil deeds of Hojeda. These were in a certain farm or village near Xaragua. For all were scattered among the Indian villages, to be fed and maintained by the natives, which could not be done if they all remained together. As these men refused their approval when they were incited, either by letters or by word of mouth, or because they had among them some one who was obnoxious to Hojeda in times past, he arranged one night, in concert with those who had joined him, to attack the loyal men and wreak his vengeance on them, or do them some other injury; and this was done, with the result that several men were killed and wounded on both sides.

This caused great scandal in the land, among Indians as well as Christians, so that disturbances even worse than those of Roldán, recently appeased, would have arisen if God, using the same Roldán as His instrument, had not obviated the danger. Roldán now returned from Santo Domingo to Xaragua. Either because the Admiral suspected that Hojeda would return and cause injury, both to Christians and Indians, and wished to be certain that he had left the island; or because he had received intelligence from the Christians who remained loyal of what was taking place, for they sent messages by Indians every eight days, he finally despatched Roldán to Xaragua, who heard on the road of the scandals and mischief done by Hojeda, and of the object he announced. Roldán then sent to one Diego de Escobar, a leading man among those who had always followed him, ordering him to collect as large a force as possible from among those who had not been influenced by Hojeda, and to come with them to Xaragua. He collected all he could from the villages in which the Christians were scattered, and both arrived at Xaragua on two successive days. Hojeda had by that time returned to his ships.

Francisco Roldán wrote a letter to Hojeda, pointing out the scandals, deaths, and mischief he had caused, the disservice that the Sovereigns would receive from such conduct, the disturbance caused in the colony, the good will which the Admiral entertained towards him, and urging him not to adopt a course which would cause loss to all. In order that the evils might be forgotten, as what was done could not be helped, he proposed that Hojeda should at least come and excuse himself. Hojeda would not place himself in such peril, for he knew Roldán to be an astute and resolute man, and with no small intelligence. Roldán then sent Diego de Escobar to confer with Hojeda, who was not less able than the other two. I knew him well during many years. Escobar set before Hojeda the heinous character of what he had done as strongly as he could, and urged him to come to Roldán. Hojeda replied that it was what he wished to do. Escobar returned without having been able to make a definite arrangement. But Roldán, believing that Hojeda would agree, sent one Diego de Truxillo, who, as soon as he came on board the ship, was seized and put in irons. Hojeda then landed and marched to Xaragua with twenty armed men. He found there one Toribio de Linares, whom I also knew well. He was seized and taken to the ships, where he was put in irons. These proceedings were reported by the Indians to Roldán, who was then at a distance of a league from Xaragua. Roldán quickly set out in pursuit with the men he had with him, well equipped, but Hojeda was already out of his reach. He then sent one Hernando de Estepa, whom I also knew well, to whom Hojeda said that unless one Juan Pintor, who had left the ship, was given up (a man whom I also knew, and who only had one hand), he swore he would hang the two prisoners he had in irons. What harm had these done to merit hanging, because Juan Pintor had deserted! Hojeda got under weigh with his ships, and proceeded along the coast to some villages and a province called Cahay, where there is a charming country and people, ten or twelve leagues from Xaragua. Here he landed with forty men, and seized all the provisions he wanted by force, especially yams and sweet potatoes, for here are the best and finest in the island, leaving both Christians and Indians in great want. Seeing that he had made sail, Roldán sent Diego de Escobar along the sea-shore in pursuit with twenty-five men. But as they arrived at night, Hojeda had already returned to his ships. Soon afterwards, Roldán followed in pursuit with twenty men, and, having arrived at Cahay, he found there a letter which Hojeda had written to Diego de Escobar, declaring that he would hang his two prisoners if this man, Juan Pintor, was not restored. Roldán then ordered Diego de Escobar to get into a canoe, manned, as the sailors say, by Indian rowers, and to go within hail of the ships. He was to tell Hojeda, on the part of Roldán, that as he would not trust him and come to speak with him, he was willing to come to the ships, trusting in his honour, and asking that he would send a boat with this object. Hojeda perceived that his game was now made; but another thought occurred to him, which was that Francisco Roldán had brought his drums on his back, as the saying is. Hojeda sent a very good boat, for he had only one such, with eight very valiant seamen, with their lances, swords, and shields. Coming within a stone's-throw of the beach, they called out that Roldán should embark. Roldán asked, "How many did the captain say were to come with me." They answered, "Five or six men." Roldán presently ordered that Diego de Escobar should get in first, then Pero Bello, Montoya, and Hernan Brabo, and Bolaños. They would not consent that any more should get into the boat. Then Roldán said to one Pedro de Illanes that he must take him to the boat on his back, and as he wanted some one else at his side, he took another man named Salvador. Having all got into the boat, Roldán dissimulated, saying to those who were rowing that they should row towards the land. They did not wish to do so. He and his men put their hands to their swords, and laid about them with such effect that some were killed, others jumped overboard, and all were made prisoners, as well as an Indian archer kidnapped from the islands, only one escaping by swimming. They were brought on shore, and thus Hojeda was left without his best boat, of which he had much need, and also without quite so much pride and insolence. Hojeda, seeing that his artifice had failed, and his intentions were frustrated, resolved to resume the negotiation with more humility. So he got into a small boat with Juan de la Cosa, his principal pilot, a gunner, and four more, and pulled towards the shore. Francisco Roldán, knowing him to be reckless and valiant, and even thinking that he might venture to attack, got ready the large boat with seven rowers and fifteen fighting men, and a good canoe capable of holding fifteen more, all "*à pique*", as the sailors say. Being on the water, as soon as they were within hailing distance, Hojeda said that he wished to speak with Francisco Roldán. Coming nearer, Francisco Roldán asked him why he had perpetrated those scandalous and culpable acts. He replied that it was because they told him that the Admiral had given orders to apprehend him. Roldán assured him that it was false, and that the Admiral had no intention of doing him harm, but rather to help him and do him honour, and that if he would come to Santo Domingo he would find this to be true by his own experience. Finally Hojeda asked that his boat and men might be restored, no longer caring about Juan Pintor, representing that he could not return to Spain without his boat. Francisco Roldán saw the difficulty in which Hojeda was placed—for there had been a terrible gale just before, and Hojeda's largest ship had dragged her anchors, and had been driven more than two cross-bow shots nearer the shore, where the was danger of ship and crew being lost; also because if Hojeda remained on the island there would be greater confusion caused by him than had previously been caused by Roldán himself. For these reasons Roldán decided to restore the boat with the men, if Hojeda would restore the two prisoners he had seized and ill-treated. This was arranged. He departed to make an incursion, which he said he had to make, and according to what a clergyman who was with him said, and two or three other honest men who were left, the raid that he sought to make was what he intended to do against the person and affairs of the Admiral, and I firmly believe that he had means of knowing that the Sovereigns were considering the removal of the Admiral from his place. For Hojeda was in favour with the Bishop Fonseca, and, on the other hand, the same Bishop always viewed the Admiral with disfavour, justly or unjustly, as to men I say, "God knows."

According to what I suspect, when Hojeda left Española he went to load his ships with Indians, either in some part of that

island, or in the Island of San Juan,[14] or in some of the neighbour-
ing islands, for he brought to Spain and sold at Cadiz 222 slaves,
as Americo confessed in his first *Navigation*. This, with the other
injuries and outrages perpetrated on Christians and Indians by
Hojeda, was his cargo. From what has been seen in this chapter,
the falsehoods of Americo are apparent, and the tyrannies committed in this his first voyage, when he accompanied Hojeda, as
well as the way in which he confused the events of the two
voyages, are now made as evident as that the sun shines. Americo
says, respecting the scandals of Hojeda which took place during
the first voyage, but which he places in the second, as follows:

"We departed, and, for the sake of obtaining many things of
which we were in need, we shaped a course for the island of
Antiglia, being that which Christopher Columbus discovered a
few years ago. Here we took many supplies on board, and remained two months and 17 days. Here we endured many dangers
and troubles from the same Christians who were in this island
with Columbus. I believe this was caused by envy; but to avoid
prolixity I will refrain from recounting what happened. We
departed from the said island on the 22nd of July."

All this is false. He says that he does not describe the troubles
they suffered, to avoid prolixity, giving to understand that they
suffered unjustly; and he does not tell the cause, or what were the
outrages that they committed. Moreover, to place these scandals
in the second voyage is also false, as has already been sufficiently
shown. To state that the date of departure was the 22nd of July is
still more false. For that date was almost at the end of February in
the year 1500, and I even believe in March, as appears from the
letters which I saw and had in my possession. I know the handwriting of Francisco Roldán, who wrote every eight or fifteen days
to the Admiral, when he went to watch Hojeda. The fact is that

the date which should belong to the second he put in the first voyage; and the outrages and harm those who were with him did in the first, he referred to as injuries done to them, without provocation, in the second voyage.

APPENDIX F

VOYAGE OF HOJEDA, 1498-1500
(*From Navarrete*, III, pp. 3-11)

Between 1825 and 1837, in Madrid, Don Martín Fernández de Navarrete publishes a monumental work entitled Colección de los viajes y descubrimientos que hicieron por mar los Españoles desde fines del siglo XV, con varios documentos inéditos concernientes a la historia de la marina castellana y de los establecimientos españoles de Indias. *In volume III (pp. 3-11), the historian reconstructs the voyage undertaken by Alonso de Hojeda and Juan de la Cosa in 1498-1500, in which Vespucci also took part, and which he would refer to also in his first familiar letter to Lorenzo di Pierfrancesco de' Medici.*

In December 1498 the news arrived of the discovery of Paria. The splendid ideas of the discoverer touching the beauty and wealth of that region were presently made known, and the spirit of maritime enterprise was revived with renewed vigour. Some of those who had sailed with the Admiral, and had benefited by his instruction and example, solicited and obtained from the Court licenses to discover, at their own proper cost, the regions beyond what was already known, paying into the Treasury a fourth or fifth part of what they acquired.

The first who adventured was Alonso de Hojeda, a native of Cuenca. Owing to his energy and the favour of the Bishop Don Rodriguez de Fonseca, he soon collected the funds and the crews necessary for the equipment of four vessels in the Port of Santa

Maria, where Juan de la Cosa resided, a great mariner according to popular ideas, and not inferior to the Admiral himself in his own conceit. He had been a shipmate and pupil of the Admiral in the expedition of Cuba and Jamaica. This man was the principal pilot of Hojeda. They also engaged others who had been in the Paria voyage. Among the other sharers in the enterprise, the Florentine Americo Vespucci merits special mention. He was established in Seville, but became tired of a mercantile life, and entered upon the study of cosmography and nautical subjects, with the desire of embracing a more glorious career. Perhaps this passion was excited by intercourse with the Admiral in the house of Juan Berardi, a merchant, and also a Florentine, and owing to his having become acquainted through this house with the armaments and provisions for the Indies, so that he desired to place his services at the disposal of the commander of the present enterprise.

With such useful companions Hojeda put to sea on the 18th[15] or the 20th of May 1499.[16] They touched at the Canaries, where they took in such supplies as they needed, and entered on the ocean voyage from Gomera, following the route of the last voyage of the Admiral, for Hojeda was in possession of the marine chart which Columbus had drawn. At the end of twenty-four days they came in sight of the continent of the new world, further south than the point reached by the Admiral, and apparently on the coast of Surinam. They sailed along in sight of the coast for nearly 200 leagues, from the neighbourhood of the equator to the Gulf of Paria, without landing. In passing, besides other rivers, they saw two very large ones which made the sea water to be fresh for a long distance, one coming from south to north, which should be the river now called Essequibo in Dutch Guiana, and which was for some time called the *Rio Dulce.* The course of the other was from west to east, and may have been the Orinoco, the waters of which flow for many leagues into the sea without mixing with the salt water. The land on the coast was, generally, low and covered with very dense forest. The currents were exceedingly strong towards the N.E., following the general direction of the coast.

The first inhabited land seen by our navigators was the island of Trinidad, on the south coast of which they saw a crowd of astonished people watching them from the shore. They landed at three different places with the launches well provisioned, and twenty-two well-armed men. The natives were Caribs, or Cannibals, of fine presence and stature, of great vigour, and very expert in the use of bows and arrows, and shields, which were their proper arms. Although they showed some reluctance to come near the Spaniards at first, they were very soon satisfied of the friendly intentions of the strangers, and bartered with them amicably. Thence they entered the Gulf of Paria, and anchored near the river Guarapiche, where they also saw a populous village of peaceful Indians near the shore. They opened communications with the inhabitants, and, among other presents, received from them a kind of cider made of fruits, as well as some fruit like *mirabolans*, of exquisite flavour, and here some pearls were obtained. They saw parrots of various colours; and they parted company with these people on friendly terms. Hojeda says that they found traces of the Admiral having been in the island of Trinidad, near the Dragon's Mouth, which circumstance was carefully omitted by Vespucci.

Having passed the mouth of the terrible strait, Hojeda continued his discovery along the coast of the mainland as far as the Gulf of Pearls or Curiana, visiting and landing on the island of Margarita, which is in front, as he knew that Columbus had only sighted it in passing. In passing he noticed the islets called *Los*

Frailes, which are nine miles to the east, and north of Margarita, and the rock *Centinela*. Thence he stood in shore by the cape *Isleos* (now called *Codera*), anchoring in the road which he called *Aldea vencida*. He continued to coast along from port to port, according to the expression of the pilot Morales, until he reached the *Puerto Flechado*, now *Chichirivichi*, where he seems to have had some encounter with the Indians, who wounded twenty-one of his men, of whom one died, as soon as he was brought to be cured, in one of the coves that are between that port and the *Vela de Coro*, where they remained twenty days. From this place they shaped a course for the island of Curaçao, which they called *Isla de los Gigantes*, where Americo supposed there was a race of uncommon stature. Perhaps he did not understand the expressions of horror with which the natives referred to the Caribs, and this sufficed to make Vespucci assert that he had seen Pontasiloas and Antaeus. They then crossed to a land which they judged to be an island, distant ten leagues from Curaçao, and saw the cape forming a peninsula, which they named *San Roman*, probably because it was discovered on the 9th of August, on which the feast of that saint is kept. Having rounded the cape, they entered a great gulf, on the eastern side of which, where it is shallow and clear of rocks, they saw a great village, with the houses built over the water, on piles driven into the bottom, and the people communicated from one to the other in canoes. Hojeda named it the Gulf of Venice, from its similarity to that famous city in Italy. The indians called it the Gulf of Coquibacoa, and we know it now as the Gulf of Venezuela. They explored the interior, and discovered, as it would seem, on the 24th of August, the lake and port of San Bartolomé,[17] now the lake of Maracaibo, where they obtained some Indian women of notable beauty and disposition. It is certain that the natives of this country had the fame of being more beautiful and gracious than those of any other part of that continent. Having explored the western part of the gulf, and doubled the Cape of Coquibacoa, Hojeda and his companions examined the coast as far as the Cabo de la Vela, the extreme point reached in this voyage. On the 30th of August they turned on their homeward voyage for Española or Santo Domingo, and entered the port of Yaquimo on the 5th of September 1499, with the intention of loading with brasil wood, according to what Don Fernando Columbus says.

Here Hojeda had those disputes with Roldán which are referred to by our historians, but, finally, with leave from that chief, Hojeda removed his ships to Surana, in February 1500. According to Vespucci, in his letter to Medici, they navigated from Española in a northerly direction for 200 leagues, discovering more than a thousand islands, most of them inhabited, which would probably be the Lucayas, although those are not nearly so numerous. On one of these he says that they violently seized 232 persons for slaves, and that from thence they returned to Spain by the islands of the Azores, Canary and Madeira, arriving in the Bay of Cadiz in the middle of June 1500, where they sold many of the 200 slaves that arrived, the rest having died on the voyage. The truth of these events is not very certain, but it is certain that the profit of the expedition was very small. According to the same Vespucci, deducting costs, not more than 500 ducats remained to divide among 55 shareholders, and this when, besides the price of the slaves, they brought home a quantity of pearls, worthy of a place in the royal treasury, of gold and some precious stones, but not many, for, imitating badly the acts of the Admiral, the desire to push on for discovery was greater than that for the acquisition of riches.

NOTES

1. The rubrics introducing each of the Familiar Letters and the Ridolfi Fragment belong to the manuscript tradition.

2. June 1500.

3. If, as it seems, the reference is to Alonso de Hojeda's expedition, there were four caravels and Amerigo was only one of the "pilots" appointed as an aid to Juan de la Cosa and others (see Navarrete, II, p. 320). According to Magnaghi (1924, II, p. 126 ff.), after the landing at 5 degrees north, Vespucci supposedly continued southeast with two caravels, while Hojeda and de la Cosa immediately headed northwest.

4. One of the Canary Islands, southwest of Tenerife and northeast of Hierro.

5. The site of the landing corresponds to a point on the coast of French Guiana, between 4 and 5 degrees north.

6. Near the mouth of the Amazon River.

7. The *Sinus Magnus* of ancient cartography; that is, the easternmost part of the Indian Ocean, then considered an enclosed sea. Ptolemy placed Cattigara, a Sinitic town later identified as Malacca, on the western coast of the Indian Ocean at 8 degrees 50′ south.

8. "It is . . . likely that Vespucci, once in the mouth of the Amazon, southwest of the island of Caviana, was alluding to the river's main left branch and to its other main estuary, which goes from South to North

and lies to the right of the Ihla dos Porcos [Isle of Pigs]" (Magnaghi 1924, II, p. 146).

9. Vespucci supposedly deserves credit for discovering the Amazon River, which he explored upstream for about 100 kilometers.

10. The Guiana stream, which forks near the southernmost point in this voyage, the Cape of São Roque (Brazil). Vespucci is the first to have reported it.

11. The Strait of Messina, at the northeast tip of Sicily.

12. Below, 6 ½ degrees; it corresponds to the latitude of the Cape of São Roque (see note 10 above).

13. The stars of the Ursa Minor, in particular the two that follow the North Star.

14. Mandelbaum translation.

15. The Southern Cross.

16. An error that recurs in the entire manuscript tradition. The latitute should be 41 ½ degrees as can be inferred from the calculation that follows in the text.

17. Johann Müller from Königsberg, in Latin Johannes Regiomontanus (1436-76), a famous mathematician and astronomer, who is mentioned here as the author of the *Ephemerides astronomicae (Almanac)* for the years 1476-1506. These astronomical tables refer not to the meridian of Ferrara (as in the *Tabulae tabularum* by Giovanni Bianchini, Müller's teacher), but to that of Nüremberg, where the *Ephemerides* were first published.

18. The so-called *Tablas alfonsíes*, after Alfonso X (el Sabio), King of Castile and Leon (1221-84). They were written in Toledo in 1252.

19. One would probably expect 3 degrees (Magnaghi 1924, II, p. 154), but the calculation that follows makes sense only if it refers to the 5½ hours mentioned below. According to J.W. Stein, Vespucci is just repeating Columbus's calculations for the longitude of the island of Saona (Dominican Republic).

20. Below, 84 degrees. On the somehow mysterious discrepancies in these calculations see Magnaghi 1924, II, p. 151.

21. The ninth-century astronomer Aḥmad ibn Muḥammad ibn Kathīr, called Al-Fārganī, mentioned here as the author of the *Liber aggregationum stellarum* (1493).

22. Trinidad, so christened by Columbus on 31 July 1498.

23. The similarity with Simone dal Verde (p. 80) is remarkable, given the fact that dal Verde totally relies on Columbus; see also Scillacio (p. 87) and Fernando Columbus (I, p. 268).

24. The westernmost branch of the Orinoco River. The Gulf of Paria (Venezuela) was discovered by Columbus, who arrived there during his third voyage, setting foot for the first time on the American continent.

25. Another similarity with Simone dal Verde's second letter (p. 82), later made more explicit in the Soderini Letter (see VI, p. 80).

26. A variety of plum; in particular, the myrobalane is an ovoidal drupe from Combreatceous (America) or Euphorbiaceous (Africa) trees, used pharmacologically both as a laxative and an astringent. The noun, a cognate of Pliny's "myrobalanum," is already adapted to the new American setting by Michele de Cuneo (ll. 244-45); but also see Columbus's third

voyage (in *Textos*, p. 230): "they found plenty of fruits, and tasty grapes, and delicious myrobalanes."

27. "American lions," or pumas.

28. An iguana (in which case the "8 braccia" is hyperbolic), or an anaconda.

29. According to Humboldt (IV, p. 197) and Magnaghi (1924, II, p. 156), the episode is likely to be reflected in the toponym Puerto Flechado (Stricken Port, probably today's Chichiriviche, Venezuela), which appeared on the maps starting with Juan de la Cosa's.

30. As Magnaghi remarks (1924, II, p. 156), in Juan de la Cosa's map, next to Puerto Flechado is a site called Aldea Quemada (Burnt Village).

31. The Isle of the Giants (Curaçao), so indicated in Juan de la Cosa's map, in the Soderini Letter (VI, p. 84), and in one of the *probanzas* (pieces of evidence) given to the *Fiscal* (the prosecutor) by Alonso de Hojeda and Andrés de Morales (Navarrete, II, p. 319).

32. Characters in classical mythology, possibly filtered through Dante: see *Inferno* IV, 124 and XXI, 112-45, respectively. On the representation of Indians as giants, see Gerbi, p. 56, note 1 (and index).

33. Venice lends its name to both the gulf and the region of Venezuela (literally 'little Venice'). Here, however, the name is applied not to the mainland but to the island of Aruba, situated at the entrance of the Gulf of Maracaibo; by "mistake" the name will be transferred to a site on the coast in Juan de la Cosa's map (Magnaghi 1924, II, p. 158).

34. Large cargo and battleships used by both the Genoese and the Portuguese since the thirteenth century.

35. The languages originating with the confusion of Babel were thought to

be seventy or seventy-two, as attested to by a tradition, both Judaic and patristic, still alive in seventeenth-century philosophy.

36. In fact, already eight years before the date of the letter, unless it relates to the period between 1493 (the date of the Almirante's return to Spain and of the letter announcing the discovery) and 1499 (the date of the departure of Vespucci's expedition). In any case, the reading is common to the entire manuscript tradition, thus going back at least to its first instance.

37. Castile is used here to denote Spain in general.

38. The Islas Lucayas, or present-day Bahamas.

39. Latitude of Cadiz, today determined as 36 degrees 32'.

40. Possible allusion to the preparations for Diego de Lepe's second expedition, mentioned also in an official document dated 15 November 1500 (Navarrete, II, pp. 57-58). The expedition did not take place then because of the captain's death.

41. Ptolemy's Taprobane, identified sometimes with Ceylon (Sri Lanka) and sometimes with Sumatra.

42. The Bay of Bengal.

43. Manuel I, King of Portugal from 1495 to 1521.

44. It is the first expedition of Vasco da Gama, who sailed from Lisbon on 9 July 1497, hence three years before Vespucci's return.

45. The Portuguese allegedly remained in Calicut (on the western coast of India) from 10 May to 25 August 1498. Calicut, however, lies southeast, and not west, of the Indus River.

46. The fleet, commanded by Pero Álvares Cabral and headed toward Calicut, had sailed from Lisbon in March of 1500. It was made up of 13 vessels, "but one of them, captained by Gaspar de Lemos, was allegedly sent back to Lisbon to report on the discovery of Brazil" (Ramusio, I, p. 623 note 1).

47. The 28th, according to the reading of both the Vaglienti and Ridolfi codices. On these manuscript codices see the introduction, pp. xxvii–xxviii and xxxiv, respectively.

LETTER II

1. A no longer extant letter.

2. Manuel I.

3. 13 May 1501.

4. Ethiopia refers here to a region in Western Africa, in particular Senegal and Guinea. Ptolemy made a distinction between *Aethiopia interior* and *Aethiopia sub Aegypto*.

5. Cape Verde, placed today at 14 degrees 41' north, is on the same meridian of Gomera (17 degrees 15' west of Greenwich, in the Canary Islands).

6. The reference is to Pero Álvares Cabral's fleet, which sailed from Lisbon on 9 March 1500, hence not fourteen but sixteen months before the date of the letter.

7. See the preceeding note; once "April" is replaced by "March," the identification of the year with 1499 implies a dating with a "Florentine" imprint (see introduction, pp. xxvi ff.).

8. See note 5 above. The reference is to the first meridian of Ptolemaic tradition, situated between Tenerife and Grand Canary, at about 6 degrees west.

9. But a south-southeast direction seems however necessary. Pohl (p. 226, n. 3) argues that Cabral's vessels could have headed west after reaching Cape Balmas, or Cape Lopez (in present-day Gabon), also because the distance of seven hundred leagues would otherwise be excessive.

10. The "four miles" in the first Familiar Letter are thus updated; see I, p. 4 : "four leagues (or sixteen miles)." Assuming that the equation (1 degree=16 ⅔ leagues) is maintained (see I, p. 8), the importance of this updating should consist in its measure of the earth's circumference which is not far from its actual value (Pohl, p. 227, n. 4).

11. If Cabral landed at around 17 degrees south (hence further east than the Cape of São Roque), Vicente Yáñez Pinzón had already reached 8 degrees latitude in the Southern hemisphere, and this explains the remark on the continuity of the Brazilian coast.

12. 2 May 1500.

13. In fact only four; the fifth vessel had already disappeared near the Cape Verde Islands.

14. In fact seven; besides the five already sunk, Gaspar de Lemos's vessel, which returned to Portugal to announce the discovery of Brazil, should be kept in mind.

15. The longitude is excessive here, even assuming as reference the meridian of Cape Verde (Pohl, p. 227, note 5). In any case, the Cape of Good Hope is on the meridian of Alexandria also in Ramusio's map (V, p. 38, note 2 to p. 39).

16. The mythical Christian King, whose seat was at times located in Asia

(particularly India, due to the presence of groups of Nestorian Christians, whose origin was linked to the preaching of the Apostle Thomas), at times in Ethiopia (as in most 16th-century sources, which implied the identification of Prester John with the Monophysite king of Aksum); see below note 26.

17. According to Strabon's *Geography* (II, 5, 26), also referred to, in the 16th century, by Leo Africanus (see Ramusio, I, pp. 19 and 21).

18. *Miticale* (a Portuguese word of Arab origin) designated a gold coin with a weight of 4.25 grams. *Castellana* was a Spanish gold coin weighing 4.6 grams; it was so called because of the castle that appeared on one of its sides.

19. The naïveté is only apparent, since the problem of the name had been clearly stated by Pliny (*Naturalis Historia*, VI, 28), and is cited as such by other voyagers (see for instance Ramusio, II, p. 63 and n. 1)

20. Perhaps Diogo Dias's vessel, "which reached the mouth of Mecca's Strait" (Ramusio, I, p. 652).

21. The Mameluke Sultan of Egypt, Malīk al-Ashraf.

22. Gaspar da India; born in Alexandria to Polish-Jewish parents, he later converted to Islam. In 1498 he was turned over to Vasco da Gama, baptized (hence the alternative name Gaspar da Gama), and taken to Lisbon.

23. Until Diego Lopez de Sequeyra's voyage (1508), the position of Malacca must have been so uncertain that it was located at 33 degrees south (see p. 93, and p. 194 note 49). The same holds true for the reference to the ancient Gedrosia, the Asian region known for its aridity, and corresponding to today's southeastern Iran and western Baluchistan.

24. He first went to Lisbon with Vasco da Gama (see note 22 above).

25. 13 September 1500.

26. It replaces the manuscript's "St. Mark." The confusion with the evangelist of Alexandria (whose remains had been in Venice since 829) can be explained by the more general confusion between the two sects inspired by the two saints: Jacobites, or Eutychian Monophysites from Syria; and 'Christians of Saint Thomas,' or Nestorians. It should be added that a 'western' trend was confirmed by the presence at Edessa (Syria) of the cult of St. Thomas's relics, and that a similar shift from east to west had already taken place for the Nestorian (but by the seventeenth century certainly Ethiopian and Coptic) Prester John. In any case, Thomas was buried not in "Emparlicat" (probably a variant of "Perlicat": Pulicat, on the eastern coast of India, not far from Madras), but in nearby Mailapur.

27. For the alternation with Ceylon see the first Familiar Letter (I, p. 175 note 41).

28. However, Cabral did not reach the Moluccas (mentioned here for the first time). Evidently, Gaspar da Gama is adding to the account of Cabral's voyage the information he had on the lands east of India.

29. See note 14 above.

30. The cargo captained by Sancho de Tovar.

31. See note 13 above.

32. See note 20 above.

33. On Simone dal Verde, see introduction p. xxvi , and *Raccolta*, III, vol. II, pp. 79-82.

NOTES

LETTER III

1. 22 July 1502 (Magnaghi 1924, I, pp. 34 and 51 note 1).

2. The second Familiar Letter.

3. In the neutral sense of 'unknown land.' The landing took place on 7 August according to the *Mundus Novus* (see V, p. 47), but on the 17th of the same month according to the Soderini Letter (see VI, p. 87). Magnaghi (1924, II, pp. 209-10) suggests the date of 16 August and a southern latitude of 6 degrees, corresponding to the latitude of the Cape of São Roque, the southernmost point reached during the first voyage.

4. If one keeps to the tradition of the Familiar Letters, according to which the Portuguese voyage is preceded by only one Spanish voyage, the plural implies a reference to other letters regarding voyages 'by way of land' to Spain, Portugal, or even within Italy. The voyage from Lisbon to Cape Verde, mentioned by the preceeding letter, is to be considered merely an intermediate stage.

5. At the latitude of Puerto Santa Cruz (Humboldt, V, p. 20, note 2). On 28 February 1500, at the latitude of 49 degrees south, Puerto San Julián (on the southern coast of Argentina) might well have been recognized and christened; it is the same port where Magellan's fleet spent the winter of 1520 (Magnaghi 1924, II, pp. 221-25; Pohl, p. 123 and note 5).

6. From August 1501 to June 1502, when the return voyage begins.

7. The angle formed on a sphere by two intersecting circumferences.

8. The latitude of Lisbon (in fact 38 degrees 42′ north). See *Mundus Novus*, p. 54.

9. See p. 174, note 27.

10. Already for Columbus this is a typical trait of the Cannibals, as opposed to the "Taínos" of Española. Indeed, the detail relates here to the Tupí-Guaraní of Brazil.

11. See the description in Vaz de Caminha on the discovery of Brazil (c. 2v): "they had their lower lips pierced, and in them they had white bones as long as a palm is wide, and as thick as a spool of cotton, and as pointed at their ends as a needle."

12. In fact a little less than 131.

13. In the *canzone* for the crusade against the Turk, "O aspettata in ciel beata e bella," ("O soul awaited in heaven, blessed and beautiful"). See Petrarch, *Rerum Vulgarium Fragmenta*, XXVIII, l. 60: "ma tutti colpi suoi commette al vento" ("but entrusts all their blows to the wind," Durling translation).

14. Perhaps this should be related to a custom described also by Fernando Columbus (II, p. 32): "Others are burned in the house where they die, and when they see one at the point of death they do not let him die, but they strangle him, and this is done to the Caciqui."

15. Same as cassia.

LETTER IV

1. According to the Soderini Letter (VI, p. 91) this same coast was followed for about twenty leagues.

2. In fact only eleven, from 10 May 1501 to 7 April 1502 (see VI, p. 91)

3. A quotation from the book of the *Apocalypse* (7: 9), as the *Mundus Novus* in fact specifies (V, p. 48).

4. Probably in the sense that use produces a habit that can be considered 'second nature': ὅμοιον γάρ πι τὸ 'ἔθος ("habit is something like nature"). See Aristotle, *Rhetoric* I, 11, 1370a, 7-8; *Nicomachean Ethics* II, i, 1103a ff. There is a similar approach in the Thomistic commentary to the *Ethics* (II, lect. 6, n. 315): "consuetudo in naturam vertitur" ("habit becomes nature").

5. Relative to the equinox, hence constant in time. But according to the data reported here, the distance in longitude between Lisbon and Ferrara comes to 40 degrees, "whereas it is only 20 degrees" (Magnaghi 1937, p. 619).

6. See the first Familiar Letter (I, p. 8, and notes 17-18), where Johannes Regiomontanus's *Almanach* is similarly related to Ferrara. Giovanni Bianchini (Blanchinius), a professor of astronomy, published in Venice in 1495 his *Tabulae celestium motuum*, referring them to the meridian of Ferrara, where he taught. Abraham Zacuto's *Tabulae*, in the translation of his student José Vizinho, were instead published in Leiria (Portugal) where the Sephardic doctor, who had taught in Salamanca (taken as meridian of reference), found shelter in 1492 while fleeing the anti-semitic laws promulgated by the Catholic Sovereigns. On this Jewish figure, still active in 1510, see Magnaghi 1934, pp. 161 ff.

7. See p. 176, note 4.

8. A promontory in Morocco.

9. The geographical context allows the hypothesis of "Anghille" being a mistake for *Argila*, or *Arzila* (Asilah, in Morocco). The identification previously proposed in Formisano 1985, p. 257 ("Cabo de Agulhas, at the southernmost end of South Africa") is thus corrected.

10. After Sanhadja, the Arabic name for one of the major subdivisions, from Mauretania to Senegal, of Berbers. The desert of the same name in-

cludes the ex-Spanish part of the Sahara and Mauretania. Here Zanaga refers to a site near the mouth of the similarly named river (in today's Cameroon).

11. The river is in today's Guinea-Bissau; Sierra Leone is also mentioned in the Soderini Letter as "a coastal land of Ethiopia." (see VI, p. 92).

12. Probably read "[usa]," literally 'uses with,' in the sense of 'has sex with.'

13. Probably "two different [points]."

14. In this sense the text is very close to the third Familiar Letter (see III, p. 30); in *Mundus Novus*, the remark belongs conversely to the last section (see V, p. 54).

15. But see *Mundus Novus* (V, p. 54). The latitude of Lisbon is today plotted at 38 degrees 43' north.

16. Probably "that [it was a fourth] part of the world or [maximum] orbit" (see III, p. 30: "a quarter of the world," and p. 37: "one quarter of the terrestrial world").

17. A pun in the Italian text: *metamastico* refers both to *metamatico* (a vernacular form of *matematico*/mathematician), and the verb *masticare* (literally to "chew," in the sense of "having a smattering").

18. Probably "[slave's] head," for "a slave."

LETTER V

1. Manuel I.

2. See III, p. 29 (and note 3) "a new land." Here, however, the *Mundus*

Novus is not only an "unknown world" (V, p. 46), but it identifies a continent distinct from Europe, Asia, or Africa (see below).

3. See Waldseemüller's suggestion, *Appendix D, p.* 116 : "Inasmuch as both Europe and Asia received their names from women . . ."

4. 13 May in the second Familiar Letter (II, p. 19), 10 May in the Letter to Piero Soderini (VI, p. 86).

5. The 1505 edition continues with: "abeundo, terras perlustrando et redeundo" ("going, exploring the land, and coming back"); that is, the twenty months refer to the entire length of the voyage, including the return, taking us back to January 1502. According to the Letter to Piero Soderini (VI, p. 92), Vespucci arrived on 7 September 1502; but see p. 180, note 1.

6. On the first meridian, see p. 174, note 8.

7. See p. 177, note 4. But in Ptolemaic geography Cape Verde is instead called the Western Horn [Corno d'Occidente] (Magnaghi 1924, I pp. 74-75).

8. Bezeguiche is present-day Gorée, near Cape Verde.

9. Southeast wind; other editions read *aphricus* (i.e. *africus,* "south by southwest wind"), which is the only possible course (see III, p. 29: "we sailed a course southwest by south").

10. But below: "sixty-seven days"; "sixty-four days" in the third Familiar Letter (III, p. 29).

11. See preceding note.

12. See p. 176, note 3.

NOTES

13. The latitude of the Cape San Augustín: see p. 193, note 45.

14. See Ridolfi Fragment (IV, p. 37 and note 3).

15. See the Letter to Piero Soderini (VI, p. 61 and note 13).

16. See III, p. 31 (and note 10).

17. See III, p. 32 (and note 11).

18. See Ridolfi Fragment (IV, p. 42) and the Letter to Piero Soderini (VI, p. 64).

19. As the third Familiar Letter specifies (III, p. 33), it is a question of female slaves and their offspring.

20. In the third Familiar Letter (III, p. 34): "more than two hundred."

21. See the Letter to Piero Soderini (VI, p. 64 and note 17).

22. But see III, p. 33 (and note 12).

23. Southeast by ¼ south wind.

24. North by northeast wind.

25. For the details, see III, p. 32.

26. See p. 174, note 27.

27. An indirect hint of this in the first Familiar Letter (I, p. 16), "we brought back pearls." The Ridolfi Fragment comes back to this point in rather full detail (IV, p. 43).

28. But "Polycletus" was a sculptor; his name is being confused here with "Polygnotus."

29. The *Canopus* is a star of the first magnitude, originally one of the constellation of Argo.

30. What will further on be referred to as the "third journey."

31. See p. 183, note 15.

32. See below, note 1.

33. For *Africus*, see note 9 above.

34. Traditionally identified with the Veronese Dominican Fra Giovanni del Giocondo (1433-1515), an architect and humanist who had in this era gone to Paris for the building of the Pont de Notre-Dame. Vespucci may have known him there, through his uncle Guidantonio's embassy (see introduction, p. xxxv), or in Florence, where the Veronese friar was living around 1490, gaining contact with Lorenzo the Magnificent. But perhaps it is correct to keep to the lower-case spelling of early editions, in the reading *jocundus interpres*, i.e. "a pleasant, or delightful interpreter" (see Magnaghi 1924, I, p. 62).

LETTER VI

1. Not Fernando VI but, according to the Castile & León line of succession, Fernando V, who was only a regent after the deaths of both Isabella (26 November 1504) and her son-in-law (25 November 1506). It is also true, though, that for an "Italian of Seville" the kingdom of Castile could represent all of Spain (see *Mundus Novus*, p. 54: "the Most Serene King of the Spains").

2. Manuel I.

NOTES

3. Latin grammar. Codex 2649 of the Biblioteca Riccardiana in Florence contains a Vespucci autograph with translation exercises from Italian into Latin; it is the only document we have of the future navigator's studies.

4. Amerigo's paternal uncle, born in 1434. A scholar of Greek and Latin, he was prominent in Marsilio Ficino's Academy. After becoming a follower of Savonarola's, in 1497 he entered the Dominican convent of St. Mark in Florence, where he became priest in 1499. He died in the Dominican convent of Fiesole in 1514.

5. See Petrarch, *Rerum Vulgarium Fragmenta* I, 4: "quand'era in parte altr'uom da quel ch'i' sono" ("when I was in part another man from what I am now," Durling translation).

6. In fact Catullus to Cornelius Nepos, in the dedicatory poem of his *libellum* (ll. 3-4): ". . . namque tu solebas / meas esse aliquid putare nugas" (". . . for you have been accustomed / to think that there is something in my trifles," Sisson translation).

7. By 10 March 1492 Vespucci is in Seville, where he works for Giannotto Berardi, a trade agent for Lorenzo di Pierfrancesco de' Medici. The four years thus refer to the period 1492-96, the departure for the first voyage being dated here 10 May 1497.

8. Erroneous reading common to the entire manuscript tradition, since the voyage, according to the narrative of the text, lasted eighteen months.

9. Dante, *Inferno* XXVI, 114: ". . . del mondo sanza gente" (". . . of the world that is unpeopled," Mandelbaum translation).

10. See p. 177, note 8.

11. Latitude and longitude seem to indicate a landing near Trujillo (Gulf of

Honduras). But "assuming the results of the computation based on the coordinates and the direction followed, the distance should be 1600 leagues, and the landing should be much further south, more or less at 6 degrees north toward the northernmost end of the French Guiana" (Magnaghi 1924, II, pp. 69-70).

12. It is the beginning of a long description that well suits the cannibals of the Guiana (see preceeding note), rather than the population of Honduras. From the outset, this description appropriates themes that appear to be already codified in the early literature about America. Many of these themes can be found in Vespucci's Familiar Letters and the Ridolfi Fragment, as well as in the *Mundus Novus*. Also remarkable are the verbal correspondences, interpreted by Magnaghi as the result of the work of a forger which, according to his hypothesis of a twofold fabrication, found its main source in the *Mundus Novus* (often literally translated), and its a posteriori confirmation in the Fragment.

13. See Columbus, *Diario* (16 December): "they are the handsomest men and women I have found until now. They are exceedingly white, and if they wore clothing and were protected from the sun and the air they would be almost as white as the people in Spain." See also *Mundus Novus* (V, p. 48)

14. See Columbus, *Diario* (3 December): "they carry no weapons but spears, which have a small, hardened, sharp stick on the end"; Las Casas (I, 142b): "They carried no weapons, except for spears, that is, canes with sharp ends hardened by fire, and some with a fish tooth or bone." On the general context cfr. *Carta* (p. 145): "[they] use bows and arrows made of the same canes as the weapons I described earlier, with a stick on the tip instead of iron, which they do not have"; *Diario* (12 October): "they have no iron . . . Their spears are made of wood, to which they attach a fish tooth at one end, or some other sharp thing."

15. See III, p. 32. See also Girolamo Benzoni (c. 56r): "When the women

give birth, they take their creatures to the sea, or to some river to wash them."

16. See Girolamo Benzoni (cc. 52v-53r): "With a certain herb infusion the women dispelled their pregnancies in order not to give birth." The detail, unknown to the *Mundus Novus*, can be also found in Bembo (p. 376): "if they get pregnant, with some herb appropriate to the purpose they cause a miscarriage."

17. See *Mundus Novus* (V, p. 50), and Michele de Cuneo (ll. 344-47): "The women have their breasts quite round and hard and well made . . . , nor does childbirth wrinkle their stomachs, which almost always remain tight, as do their breasts."

18. The "domus orationis" of Matthew 21: 13 (and Isaiah 56: 7).

19. Similarly in Giovanni da Verazzano (ll. 364-65): "They move their houses from one place to another according to the richness of the site and the time they have been there."

20. On this ritual see Fernando Columbus II, p. 32.

21. The manioc root and the flour extracted from it; expression from the Taíno of San Domingo. See Taviani, Scheda LXIII, pp. 329-31.

22. Cassava, the flour obtained from batatas (sweet potatoes); see Taviani, Scheda LXI, pp. 325-26. According to Las Casas, the word, also from the Taíno of San Domingo, was stressed on the next-to-last syllable (see Friederici, p. 155).

23. A term of African origin, mediated by Portuguese *(inhame)*, it generally designates an edible tuber; in Columbus, who had found similar ones in Guinea, it appears as "niames" or "mames"; see Taviani, Scheda LXII, pp. 327-28.

24. With a landing at 16 degrees north and a northwest direction, it cannot be present-day Venezuela.

25. With *almadía* (expression of Arab origin) the Portuguese designated a long and narrow boat, carved from tree trunks, in use along the coasts of Africa and Asia. In Columbus's *Diario* it is a substitute for *"canoa"* until October 25, when he adopts the native usage. The appropriate gloss appears on October 28: *"salieron dos almadías o canoas,"* next to *"canoas"* which by now was also used alone. Cf. Beccaria 1985, p. 194.

26. Hence an iguana; the description is here part of a passage that seems to derive literally from the *Libretto de tutta la navigatione de Re de Spagna* (Booklet of all the navigations of the King of Spain; see Trevisan p. 66).

27. The "bread made out of fish" is already known to Marco Polo's *Milione* (ch. 191).

28. See Michele de Cuneo, ll. 190-94: "In going and coming back, we crossed very large rivers . . . swimming, and those who could not swim had two Indians that, swimming, carried them over. Also, these Indians, out of friendship and because of some refreshments that we gave them, carried our stuff, our weapons and everything that had to be carried, upon their heads."

29. There is a similarity here with the sinners of Dante's Malebolge (see *Inferno* XXII, 25-33). The *Comedy*'s theme, however, is combined here with another, typical of Columbus's writings: see *Diario* (26 December): "I ordered that a lombard and a musket be fired, and the King was spellbound when he saw the effect of their force and what they penetrated. When people heard the shots, they fell to their knees."

30. A well-known theme of Columbus's writings; see for instance: "they believed very firmly that I with these ships and people came from

heaven," "I am bringing them with me now, and they still think I come from heaven, despite all the conversation they have had with me" (*Carta*, pp. 142 and 143); "they believe that there is a God in Heaven, and they firmly believe that we come from Heaven" (*Diario*, 11 November).

31. The expression (from the Tupí-Guaraní) is documented both in ancient (besides Vespucci, examples in Thevet, year 1558) and modern times. The gloss is also substantially correct: seers, prophets, or simply wise men, the *carabi* are first of all messengers of a word from the gods or the Beyond. As such, the expression, which is mixed here with Columbus's imagery (see preceding note), was first applied to the native shamans (in the Latin translation of the Letter the term is referred to the indians themselves), and only later to whites, as doctors and carriers of "culture."

32. It is Haiti, even though the following battle could not have taken place on the island (that is, before Hojeda's departure to Spain on 22 November 1499). A more plausible location are the Bahamas, which lay within the return route (Markham, p. xxvii). What is remarkable is the fact that this episode appropriates and amplifies what had happened in Aldea Quemada, thus, according to the first Familiar Letter, in a completely different locale (see p. 174, n. 30).

33. Ilha do Fogo (Cape Verde Islands). After identyifing the Letter's second voyage with that of Vicente Yáñez Pinzón, Humboldt (IV, p. 201) remarks that the Spanish pilot headed from Palos (or Saltes) first to the Canary Islands, then to the island of Santo Antão, north-northwest of the Ilha do Fogo (see Trevisan, p. 80).

34. Trinidad.

35. On this episode, which in fact occurred during Columbus's second voyage, see Trevisan (p. 79), Scillacio (p. 88), Michele de Cuneo (ll. 86-ff), Simone dal Verde (p. 80).

36. Instead of the cursory description of Trevisan (p. 79), where the entire situation is misunderstood, see the passage Oviedo devotes to the "herb that the Indians of Nicaragua call *yaat*, that in the jurisdiction of Venezuela is called *hado*, and in Peru *coca*" (Oviedo, VI, p. 179): "The Indians of Nicaragua and other parts where they use this herb called *yaat* have the habit, when they go to war or set out on a journey, of wearing around their neck a small bottle or other container in which they carry this herb, dried, hardened, and crushed almost into a powder. And they put in their mouth a little of it, no more than a mouthful, but they do not chew or swallow it. . . . Once they have it in their mouth, they pass it from time to time from one cheek to the other, to the effect that this herb quenches their thirst and their fatigue. And together with it, they use a certain powder made of seashells and snail shells from the seashore, which also they carry in small bottles. And with a small stick they stir it and put it from time to time into their mouth, to the effect described above."

37. Perhaps Francesco di Alamanno degli Albizzi (1433-95), here substituted for the Antaei of the first Familiar Letter (see I, p. 13 and n. 32).

38. Supposedly, then, the Spanish landed "more or less at Cape Gracias á Dios in Honduras; and amazingly they had arrived there from the last landed at place, the island of Curaçao, without the slightest mention of all the rest!" (Magnaghi 1924, I, p. 238, n. 1). A curious coincidence should, however, be accounted for: the northernmost coast reached during the the second voyage (15 degrees north) would be contiguous with the first expedition's landing point (16 degrees north).

39. In line with the manuscript tradition, a possible reading would be "sixty thousand [maravedís]."

40. Ancient name, especially Portuguese, for Española-Haiti.

41. The reference is to the rivalry between Francisco Roldán and Alonso de

Hojeda after the latter's arrival at Española on September 5 1499; the "envy" was none other than Roldán's (and Columbus's) strong opposition to letting the new arrival load brazilwood without the proper payment (see Las Casas, I, pp. 441 ff.). The Almirante was himself accused of "envy" in the *cahier de doléances* that Roldán sent to the Catholic Sovereigns, as the *Libretto* widely publicizes (see the passage in *Raccolta*, III, ii, p. 176).

42. A member of the trade circles, whose presence in Lisbon is documented for the month of May 1503 (see Magnaghi 1924, I, p. 59, n. 1).

43. Vespucci allegedly spoke of his entering Portugal's service in his letter— referred to at the beginning of the second Familiar Letter—of 8 May 1501 to Lorenzo di Pierfrancesco de' Medici. The hypothesis, advanced by Magnaghi, of Vespucci spying for Spain does not seem to have solid foundations: according to Piero Rondinelli's letter, dated Seville 3 October 1502, Amerigo's return to Spain might be explained by the lukewarm welcome he was accorded at the end of his voyage. Nor would Spain have objected to the return of a foreigner who carried precious information about the search for the southwest passage. In any case, since the middle of the sixteenth century, one good reason to go to Portugal would have been the prohibition against foreigners participating in voyages of discovery (Varela, p. 66).

44. See p. 46 (and note 8) and p. 176, note 4.

45. The testimony given by Giovanni Vespucci before the Conference of 'pilots' held in Seville in 1515 is well known: "I say that the Cape of San Augustín lies 8 degrees south from the equinoctial line . . . , and of this I have a record in his own handwriting, describing for each day which course he was sailing, and how many leagues he had made" (Navarrete, II, pp. 191-92). Naming it after St. Augustine naturally suggests 28 August, the saint's day.

46. The same also in IV, p. 37.

47. The "new land" is identified sometimes with Southern Georgia, sometimes with Patagonia, without excluding the island of Tristão da Cunha or the Falklands. This land remains mysterious, however, possibly because it is simply imaginary: "heading southeast from 32 degrees south, 50 degrees south are reached at a point that is about 25 degrees longitude from the Falklands, and almost 2,500 km. from the coasts of Patagonia" (Magnaghi 1937, p. 611).

48. 'Pilgrimage vows,' according to a custom also referred to by Ariosto (*Satire* III, 61-66); also see the vows expressed during the storm described by Columbus in his *Diario*, at the entry of February 14.

49. The latitude of Malacca, which Vespucci thought to be an island, is corrected to 3 degrees north by Ramusio (I, p. 666); see also above p. 178, n. 23.

50. Bahia de Todos os Santos. The name establishes a link with 1 November 1501 (All Saints' Day), but most of all with the church and district of Ognissanti (All Saints) in Florence, the 'little homeland' of the Vespucci family.

51. Amerigo's elder brother, and the father of Giovanni (Juan), Antonio Vespucci (1449-1534) followed in his father's footsteps, studying law at Pisa and then working in Florence as a notary. A Chancellor of the Seigneury and of the Trades, several times a Proconsul of Magistrates and Notaries, Antonio left a conspicuous number of documents on the period 1472-1532. Among the Spanish merchants he had dealings with is Juan Sanchez, brother of the same Gabriel Sanchez to whom Columbus had sent a copy of the letter announcing the discovery.

APPENDICES

1. Navarrete, i, p. 351.

2. Navarrete, iii, p. 292.

3. It has been pretended that John Cabot had sighted the continent in the previous year, but this is not so. He only sighted Cape Breton and other islands. In his second voyage he sighted the continent (1498), but the month is unknown.

4. Las Casas only knew the Latin version.

5. Juan de la Cosa was called "Vizcaíno" (Biscayan) by his contemporaries; but he was a native of Santoña, in the province of Santander, a place which was not then, and never had been, in Biscay, or in the Basque country.

6. The words "other pilots" are to be coupled with Juan de la Cosa, certainly not with Vespucci, who then went to sea for the first time, in advanced middle age, and could in no sense be called a pilot.

7. This is so. The departure, in the Latin version, is on May 20th, 1497; in the Italian it is May 10th, 1497. The date of the return is 1499 in the Latin, and 1498 in the Italian edition.

8. Columbus arrived at San Domingo, on his third voyage, after discovering Trinidad and the mainland of America, on August 31st, 1498. He found Francisco Roldán in open rebellion against his brother, the Adelantado. On October 18th, 1498, he sent five ships to Spain with a cargo of dyewood, and 600 slaves. By these ships the Admiral despatched his chart of the new discoveries, with a report, and two long letters giving an account of the rebellion of Roldán and the state of the colony. Las Casas believes that letters full of complaints of the Admiral

were also sent home by Roldán and his accomplices. The father of Las Casas, who had gone out with Columbus in 1493, returned to Spain by this opportunity.

9. Port of Jacmel in Española.

10. Juan de la Cosa.

11. Latin version. The Italian version has thirty-seven days.

12. Jacmel.

13. Juan de la Cosa.

14. Puerto Rico.

15. Vespucci.

16. Casas and Herrera.

17. Only mentioned in the three instructions given by Hojeda in his second voyage, to his nephew Pedro de Hojeda and Vergara to search for the vessel *Santa Ana*, to Vergara to go to Jamaica to buy provisions, and to Lopez to go in search of Vergara.

SELECTED BIBLIOGRAPHY

ARCINIEGAS, GERMÁN, *Amerigo and the New World*, New York, 1955.

BECCARIA, GIAN LUIGI, *Spagnolo e spagnoli in Italia. Riflessi ispanici sulla lingua italiana del Cinque e del Seicento*, Turin, 1968.

_____ , "Tra Italia Spagna e Nuovo Mondo nell'età delle scoperte: viaggi di parole," in *Lettere Italiane*, XXXVII (1985), pp. 177-203.

BEMBO, PIETRO, Excerpts from *Istoria viniziana*, in *Raccolta*, III, vol. II, pp. 373-77.

BENZONI, GIROLAMO, *La Historia del Mondo Novo*, Venice, 1572; anast. edition: Graz, 1962.

CHIAPPELLI, FREDI (ed.), *First Images of America. The Impact of the New World on the Old*, Berkeley-Los Angeles-London, 1976, 2 vols.

COLLO, PAOLO AND CROVETTO, PIER LUIGI (eds.), *Nuovo Mondo. Gli italiani (1492-1565)*, Turin, 1991.

COLUMBUS, CRISTOPHER, *Carta de D. Cristóbal Colón annunciando el descubrimiento del Nuevo Mundo, 15 febrero-14 marzo 1493*, Madrid, 1956. English tr. by Lucia Graves, in *The Columbus Papers: the Barcelona Letter of 1493, the Landfall Controversy, and the Indian Guides*, M. Obregón ed., New York, 1991.

BIBLIOGRAPHY

————— , *Diario de a bordo de Cristóbal Colón*. Estudio preliminar de Joaquín Arce. Edición de J. Arce y M. Gil Esteve, Alpignano, 1971. English transl. by Robert H. Fuson, *The Log of Cristopher Columbus*, Camden (Maine), 1987.

————— , *Textos y documentos completos, Relaciones de viajes, cartas y memoriales*, Edición de C. Varela, Madrid, 1982.

COLUMBUS, FERNANDO, *Le Historie della vita e dei fatti di Cristoforo Colombo per D. Fernando Colombo, suo figlio*, Milan, 1930, 2 vols.

FIRPO, LUIGI, *Prime relazioni di navigatori italiani sulla scoperta dell'America. Colombo, Vespucci, Verazzano*, L. Firpo ed., Turin, 1966.

FORMISANO, LUCIANO (ed.), Amerigo Vespucci, *Lettere di Viaggio*, L. Formisano ed., Milano, 1985.

————— , "Tra racconto e scrittura: la scoperta dell' America nei viaggiatori italiani del primo Cinquecento," in *Atti del IV Convegno Internazionale di Studi Colombiani (Genova 21-23 ottobre 1985)*, Genova, 1987, pp. 201-230.

————— , "'E ci chiamavano in lor lingua carabi': l'insegnamento di Amerigo Vespucci," in *Studia in honorem Prof. M. de Riquer*, IV, Barcelona, 1991, pp. 411-38.

FRIEDERICI, GEORG, *Amerikanistisches Wörterbuch und Hilfswörterbuch für den Amerikanisten*, Hamburg, 1960.

BIBLIOGRAPHY

GERBI, ANTONELLO, *La natura delle Indie Nove. Da Cristoforo Colombo a Gonzalo Fernández de Oviedo*, Milan-Naples, 1975.

HARLEY, J. BRIAN, *Maps and the Columbian Encounter*, Milwaukee, 1990.

HIRSCH, RUDOLF, "Printed Reports on the Early Discoveries and Their Reception," in Chiappelli (ed.), II, pp. 537-58.

HUMBOLDT, ALEXANDRE DE, *Examen critique de l'histoire de la géographie du Nouveau Continent et des progrès de l'astronomie aux quinzième et seizième siecles*, Paris, 1836-39, 5 vols.

LAS CASAS, BARTOLOMÉ DE, *Historia de las Indias*, in *Obras escogidas de Fray Bartolomé de Las Casas*. Texto fijado por Juan Pérez de Tudela y Emilio López Oto, vols. I-II, Madrid, 1957-61 (Biblioteca de Autores Españoles, 95-96).

Libretto de tutta la navigatione de Re de Spagna, de le isole et terreni novamente trovati, Venice, Albertino Vercellese da Lisona, 10 aprile 1504, in *Raccolta*, III, vol II, pp. 171-77. See also TREVISAN.

MAGNAGHI, ALBERTO, *Amerigo Vespucci. Studio critico con speciale riguardo ad una nuova valutazione delle fonti e con documenti inediti tratti dal Codice Vaglienti (Ricciardiano 1910)*, Rome, 1924, 2 vols.; revised and augmented edition, Rome, 1926.

_____, "Una curiosa documentazione dei servigi resi dal Portogallo alle scienze geografiche nell'Epoca delle grandi scoperte," in *Rivista Geografica Italiana*, XLI, 1934, pp. 145-68.

————, "Una supposta lettera inedita di Amerigo Vespucci sopra il suo terzo viaggio," in *Bollettino della R. Società Geografica Italiana*, Ser. VII, vol. II (1937), pp. 589-632.

————, "Ancora a proposito di una nuova supposta lettera di Amerigo Vespucci sopra un suo terzo viaggio," in *Bollettino della R. Società Geografica Italiana*, Ser. VII, vol. III, 1938, pp. 685-703.

MARKHAM, CLEMENTS R. (ed.), *The Letters of Amerigo Vespucci and Other Documents Illustrative of his Career*. Translated with Notes and an Introduction by C.R. Markham, London, 1894 (Hakluyt Society, vol. xc).

MARTINI, GIUSEPPE S. (ed.), *Mostra vespucciana. Catalogo*, Florence, 1955.

MICHELE DE CUNEO, "Michele de Cuneo a Gerolamo Annari (Savona, 15-28 ottobre 1495)," in Firpo 1966, pp. 47-76.

NAVARRETE, D. MARTÍN FERNÁNDEZ DE, "*Colección de los viajes y descubrimientos que hicieron por mar los Españoles desde fines del siglo XV, con varios documentos inéditos concernientes a la historia de la marina castellana y de los establecimientos españoles de Indias*, Madrid, 1825-1837, 3 vols.; in the notes, quotations are from *Obras de D. Martín Fernández de Navarrete*, C.S. Serrano, ed., Madrid, 1954-64, 3 vols.

NORTHUP, GEORGE TYLER, Introduction and notes to Amerigo Vespucci, *Letter to Piero Soderini, Gonfaloniere. The Year 1504*, Princeton, 1916.

BIBLIOGRAPHY

Nuova Raccolta Colombiana [NRC], Rome, 1988- .

OVIEDO, GONZALO FERNÁNDEZ DE, *Historia general y natural de las Indias*, edición y estudio preliminar de Juan Pérez de Tudela Bueso, Madrid, 1959, 5 vols. (Biblioteca de Autores Españoles, 117-21).

POHL, FREDERICK J., *Amerigo Vespucci, Pilot major*, New York, 1945.

POZZI, MARIO (ed.), *Il Mondo Nuovo di Amerigo Vespucci. Vespucci autentico e apocrifo*, Milan, 1984.

_____ , *Scopritori e viaggiatori del Cinquecento e del Seicento*, t. I [Il Cinquecento], Milan-Naples, 1991.

QUINN, DAVID B., "New Geographical Horizons: Literature," in Chiappelli (ed.), II, pp. 635-58.

Raccolta di documenti e studi pubblicati dalla R. Commissione Colombiana pel Quarto centenario dalla scoperta dell'America, Rome, 1892-96, 16 vols.

RAMUSIO, GIOVANNI BATTISTA, *Navigazioni e viaggi* [Venice, 1550 ff.], Marica Milanesi ed., Turin, 1978-88, 6 vols.

RONDINELLI, PIERO, "Lettera del 3 ottobre 1502," in *Raccolta*, III, vol. II, pp. 120-21.

SARNOW, E. AND TRÜBENBACH, K. (eds.), *"Mundus Novus." Ein Bericht Amerigo Vespuccis an Lorenzo de' Medici über seine Reise nach*

Brasilien in der Jahren 1501/02. Nach einem Exemplar der zu Rostock von Hermann Barckhusen gedruckten Folioausgabe, im Besitze der Staatbibliothek zu Frankfurt a. M., in Faksimile und mit Einleitungen herausgegeben, Strassburg im Elsass, 1903.

SCILLACIO, NICCOLÒ *De insulis Meridiani atque Indici mari nuper inventis* (Pavia, 13 dicembre 1494), in *Raccolta*, III, vol. II, pp. 83-94.

SIMONE DAL VERDE, "Lettera da Valladolid (20 marzo e 10 maggio 1494)," in *Raccolta*, III, vol. II, pp. 79-81.

————— , "Frammento di lettera da Cadice (2 gennaio 1499)," in *Raccolta*, III, vol. II, p. 82.

STEIN, J. W., *Memorie della Società Astronomica Italiana*, XXI, 1950, pp. 345-53.

TAVIANI, PAOLO EMILIO, Scheda LXI, Scheda LXII, Scheda LXIII, in NRC, I, II, pp. 325-31.

THEVET, ANDRÉ *Les singularitez de la France antarctique, autrement nommée Amerique et de plusieurs Terres et Isles decouvertes de nostre temps* [Paris, 1558]; anast. edition: Paris, 1981.

THROWER, NORMAN J.W., "New Geographical Horizons: Maps," in Chiappelli (ed.), II, pp. 659-74.

TREVISAN, ANGELO, "Lettere" (*Libretto de tutta la navigatione de Re de Spagna*), in *Raccolta*, III, vol. I, pp. 46-82.

VARELA, CONSUELO, *Cristóbal Colón y los florentinos*, Madrid, 1988.

VAZ DE CAMINHA, PERO, *Carta a el rei D. Manuel [por] Pero Vaz de Caminha*, S. Paulo, 1963.

VERAZZANO, GIOVANNI DA, "Giovanni da Verazzano a Francesco I, Re di Francia (Dieppe, 8 luglio 1524)," in Firpo 1966, pp. 161-87.

WALDSEEMÜLLER, MARTIN, *The Cosmographiae Introductio of Martin Waldseemüller in facsimile, followed by the four voyages of Amerigo Vespucci, with their translation into English; to which are added Waldseemüller's two world maps of 1507, with an introd. by Joseph Fischer and Franz von Wieser*, edited by C.G. Habermann, United States Historical Society, 1907.

INDEX

INDEX

INDEX

INDEX

INDEX

INDEX

INDEX

San Bartolomé, 168
San Domingo (Santo Domingo), 129, 152, 154, 156–58, 162, 169, 195 n. 8. See Antilia, Española
San Francisco, monastery of (in Seville), xxxviii
San Giovanni di Dio, hospital of (in Florence), xxxv
San Juan, 163
San Lucar, 127, 132, 136
San Miguel, Church of (in Seville), xxxviii
San Roman, 168
Sánchez, Gabriel, 194 n. 51
Sánchez, Juan, xxxix, 194 n. 51
Sanhadja, 182 n. 10
Santa Maria, port of (in Cadiz), xxiii, 128, 134, 165
Santander, province of Spain, 195 n. 5
Santo Antáo, 191 n. 33
Santo Domingo, see San Domingo
Santoña, 195 n. 5
Saona, 173 n. 19
Sardinia, 120
Sardinian Sea, 118
Sarmatia, 115
Sarnow, E., xxxix
Saturnian Sea (Caspian Sea), 117
Savonarola, Girolamo, 187 n. 4
Scailat, 24
Scarnai, 24
Scillacio, Niccolò, xx, 173 n. 23, 191 n. 35
Scomondel, 24
Scucan, 23
Scythians, 120
Selandia, 120
Sendacour, Jean Basin de (Johannes Basinus Sendacurius), 113
Sendacour, Mathurin Redouer de, xxi
Senegal, 176 n. 4, 182 n. 10
Sernigi, Girolamo, xxviii
Seula, 120
Seville, xxv, xxvii, xxxii, xxxvi–xxxvii, 3, 19, 85–86, 109–11, 125, 128, 134, 166, 186 n. 1, 187 n. 7, 193 nn. 43 and 45; Cathedral of, xxxviii
Sicily, 118–20, 172 n. 11; Sea of, 118–19
Sidonian Sea, 119
Sierra Leone, 39, 92–93, 183 n. 11

Simancas, General Archive of, 103
Simone dal Verde, xxvi, 26, 173 nn. 23 and 25, 179 n. 33, 191 n. 35
Simone Grineo, xxiv
Sinus Magnus, 4, 171 n.7
Sisson, Charles H., 187 n. 6
Soderini Letter, see Vespucci, Amerigo
Soderini, Piero, Gonfalonier of Justice in Florence, xxii, 57, 113, 125
Sofala, 21
Solís, Juan Díaz de, xxxviii, 107–8
South Africa, 182 n. 9
South America, xix, xxix
South Pole, 6–7, 30, 77, 90–91. See Antarctic Pole
Southern Cross, 172 n. 15
Spain, xxii–xxiii, xxxi, xxxvi, 15, 31, 58, 74, 76, 103, 115–17, 127, 133, 143, 147–49, 151, 154, 162, 169, 175 nn. 36–37, 180 n. 4, 186 n. 1, 188 n. 13, 190 n. 32, 193 n. 43, 195 n. 8;
King of, xxii, 54, 186 n. 1;
Sovereigns of, 3, 17.
See also Castile
Spallanzani, M., xxii
Stein, J.W., 173 n. 19
Stoic/Stoics, 42, 52
Strabon, 178 n. 17
Strasbourg, xxi
Strozzi family, xxviii, xxxiv
Sumatra, 25, 175 n. 41
Surana, 169
Surinam, 166
Symplegades, 119
Syria, 179 n. 26
Syrtis, 118

Tablas alfonsmes, see Alfonso X
Taíno, language of Española-San Domingo, 189 nn. 21–22
Taínos, tribe of Española-San Domingo, 181 n. 10
Tanais (present-day Don), 115–16
Tanur, 24
Taprobane, 16, 25, 120, 175 n. 41. See Ceylon
Tartars, 61
Tatar, 23
Taurus, 120

212

INDEX

INDEX